CONTENTS

WHO THIS KIT IS FOR

The *StartUp Loan Kit* is for anyone who has applied for or is considering applying for a StartUp Loan.

You might have received a loan and this kit from a loan distribution partner. Or you might have picked it up from a bookshop shelf. Either way, with a loan in your pocket and this in your hand, you have all you need to start and grow a successful business of your own.

This kit offers all the tools, tips and templates you need to take an idea or a gap in the market and turn it into a business. Doing so will be one of the best moves you've ever made!

ABOUT STARTUP LOANS

StartUp Loans are loans extended to anyone aged 18 to 24 who wants to start a business.

Launched by the government and Lord Young, this is a project to encourage thousands of young people to become their own boss.

To apply, first find the loan distribution partner that best suits your requirements. It may be an enterprise agency that's close to where you live, or a national organisation offering loans to your kind of business.

Check out the loan distribution partners at www.startuploans.co.uk

Applying is likely to involve submission of a business plan. This will be reviewed by business experts and advisors who will make a call on whether you receive the StartUp Loan. But not only do you receive the money you need to get going, you'll also be surrounded with business support and mentors to give your business every chance of success.

StartUp Loans have been launched to provide you with the capital, contacts and confidence you need when starting and growing a business.

FAQS

When can I apply?

You can apply for a StartUp Loan from 28 May 2012.

To whom do I apply?

View the StartUp Loan distribution partners at www.startuploans.co.uk and choose the loan provider that suits you best.

Am I eligible?

To apply for a loan, you should be older than 18 and younger than 25, living in England and thinking about starting a business.

What is the application process?

This may differ depending on the StartUp Loan provider you choose to go with but, in most cases, it will involve submitting a business plan on which your application will be based. You may also be invited to talk through your business or idea in person.

What kind of loan is it?

The StartUp Loan is a personal loan.

If I receive a StartUp Loan, what are the payback terms?

You will be required to pay back the loan within three to five years at a fixed APR (annual percentage rate) of 3% plus RPI (Retail Price Index) which is currently 3.5%.

I already have a student loan. Can I apply for a StartUp Loan as well?

Yes, you can apply for a StartUp Loan.

What else do I receive?

As well as the loan, you receive business support and mentoring and a free copy of this book, which offers all the guidance you need to start a business plus over £500-worth of offers on products from business cards to websites, netbooks and work suits.

ABOUT THE AUTHOR

Emma Jones is a business expert, author and founder of small business community Enterprise Nation. Her books include *Spare Room Start Up*, *Working 5 to 9* and *Go Global: How to take your business to the world*.

Following a five-year career at an international accounting firm, Emma started her first business at 27. That business was sold 18 months later, and the experience led to Emma's next venture, Enterprise Nation.

Its website (www.enterprisenation.com) was launched in 2006 and became the most popular site for home business owners in the UK, attracting over 100,000 visitors each month.

The site and business has grown into a friendly community of over 75,000 small business owners who help each other and benefit from the knowledge of experts through Enterprise Nation blogs, guides, books, eBooks, apps, kits and events.

Emma is also a co-founder of StartUp Britain, a national campaign to encourage more people to start a business.

EMMA JONES | @EMMALJONES

“ There is a satisfaction in creating your own enterprise that is unknown to those who work for others. **”**

– Lord Young of Graffham

FOREWORD
BY LORD YOUNG OF GRAFFHAM

As a serial entrepreneur and an occasional politician I have seen how enterprise changes people's lives, including my own. I often boast that I haven't worked since March 1961, when I left my then-employer and set up my first business. Of course, working for yourself is not always fun – it can be hard, often lonely, not always successful – but at the end of the day there is a satisfaction in creating your own enterprise that is unknown to those who work for others.

And this is not just a selfish interest. Our economy today is made up of many millions – four and a half million to be exact – of small firms, of which over a million were created in the last decade. I believe that another million will be created over the next ten years and yours could be one of them.

Some 30 years ago I created the very first business start-up programme. Some of the companies that started all those years ago are amongst the biggest in the land; but the vast majority are still small firms that have provided a lifetime's income for their founder. Our StartUp Loan programme is designed to do just that – to give you the opportunity to discover whether you have a business in you; to help you to create a business plan; and then give you a loan to get started. You will get continuing support from your mentor, and your future will be in your own hands. The limits of your business will be up to you.

Not everyone who applies will get a loan, but I believe the opportunity to meet a mentor, to talk through a possible business plan, to appreciate what is required to start, will benefit nearly all who go through the process. After all, this is nothing new – it is a tried-and-tested approach that the Prince's Trust has taken with great success for decades.

This kit is your first step to your new life. Read it and take advantage of all it offers. From this moment onwards, a new door opens.

LORD YOUNG OF GRAFFHAM | @THELORDYOUNG

> **This is one of the most rewarding and exciting journeys you can ever go on.**
>
> – James Caan

INTRODUCTION
BY JAMES CAAN

Starting your own business successfully is one of the most rewarding and exciting journeys you can ever go on. When I started my first business over 30 years ago, it paved the way for the rest of my life. I backed a lady who soon became my wife, and together we built a business that not only provided for my family, but gave me the confidence I needed to go on and launch my own business in recruitment.

To be an entrepreneur is more than having a job. It gives you the freedom to make your own mark, in the way in which you choose, and create your own path to success. It can be challenging, and exceptionally hard work, but the rewards are immeasurable. Everyone's got a personal goal, be it building the next Facebook, buying a house, paying for your student loan, or just making your first million. Entrepreneurship for me was a way to achieve my own personal aims, on my own terms, making my own mistakes but ensuring that I learnt and continued to grow as a businessman and an individual.

For me, my businesses have given me one of the greatest gifts – to be able to contribute my expertise, my capital and my time to help others. Entrepreneurship teaches you so many lessons in life that can help others succeed and for me that has been one of the best consequences of taking that step in starting my own business.

But I started on my own. With no help from anyone else. I didn't have someone to throw ideas around with, or a loan to help me on my way. I just had the bank, a gold credit card with an overdraft and my common sense. Had I had some help along the way, there would certainly have been some errors I could easily have avoided.

So that's what we have put together through this initiative. A guide to starting your own business giving you some top tips from people who have been on the journey themselves; access to expertise through the mentor scheme giving entrepreneurs someone to discuss their ideas, challenges and successes with, and ultimately a StartUp Loan to help you on your way.

For me, these are three vital ingredients to start your own business. Armed with all of these, you're already on the way to shaping your own future.

Now all you've got to do is start.

JAMES CAAN | @JAMESCAAN

LET'S GET STARTED

There has never been a better time to start a business. In 2012 record numbers of people are starting their own business and more young people than ever are considering self-employment over employment. Why? Because it's now perfectly possible to start and grow a successful business (even in your spare time and from home) on a budget and well within the means of your StartUp Loan. In this guide I'll show you how it's done.

People in their thousands are spotting gaps in the market or turning their passions, hobbies or skills into a way of making a living. They are embracing free or low-cost technology to promote themselves and make sales, with a good number of these sales coming from overseas customers. Having access to the internet means you can start a business on a Monday and be trading with the world by Wednesday.

The 20 start-up companies profiled in this book discuss how they got going and how they accessed the invaluable support that's helped them along the way. They are selling everything from large-cup lingerie to pepper grinders, rugby socks and revision apps. Their products may be different, but the owners of these businesses all talk about the opportunities available to them as young entrepreneurs and the freedom to work how and where they like.

If you'd like to experience this feeling, all you have to do is follow some basic steps: come up with an idea, do some research and marketing, offer good customer service – and you're in business! With your StartUp Loan comes ongoing advice and mentoring, so you can continue to pick up skills and meet experienced business owners who can offer advice and introductions to contacts.

In the following pages I'll walk you through the steps involved in starting your own business and making the most of your StartUp Loan.

HOW TO ACCESS YOUR OFFERS

With *The StartUp Loan Kit* comes a range of offers from top brands. These deals on everything from a website to a work suit are ideal for your new start-up.

To find out more about the offers available, and to take advantage of them, head to:

www.enterprisenation.com/slk

Here you'll find details of all partner offers. To access these simply enter the code below, select the individual offers you want, and you'll be shown the links and offer codes you need.

You don't have to access all the offers at once if you don't want to; you can come back at any time.

We'll be adding new offers throughout the year and you'll be able to access those too.

ACCESS CODE: slk0512

And that's not all ...

As well as accessing the partner offers, you can also use the above link to download templates, get hold of resources and stay bang up-to-date on the latest small business news!

eBook edition

You can download an eBook edition of this kit to read on the go on your smartphone, laptop or Kindle. Simply head to the link above or snap the QR code here.

I. PREPARE

With any undertaking, preparation is key. Whether baking a cake, going on a date or heading on holiday, time is given over to research and preparation. Starting a business is no different. Dedicate time to coming up with an idea, ensuring it's viable, and registering with the relevant bodies. These are the base ingredients required for a successful enterprise!

" Time and time again, we hear that fear is the number one reason people don't bring their business ideas to life. The only antidote to fear? Passion. "

– Melody Hossaini, founder and CEO, InspirEngage International

1. COMING UP WITH AN IDEA

Ingredient number one: a business idea! Many young people tell me they would like to start a business but what's holding them back is not having an idea. It's easy to come up with one. Ask yourself these three questions:

1. Is there a gap in the market?

Have you tried to buy something that you just can't find? Could others be looking for the same thing? If so, this presents a market opportunity. Katie Smith (page 4) spotted a gap in the market when a customer came into her mum's shop. Seeing that others might be interested in such a service, Katie's own business was born.

2. What is my passion/hobby/skill?

Many people are turning what they love into a way of making a living. Best of all, when you work on what you enjoy, doing it never really feels like work. Are you a dab hand at design? Have an eye for photography? A head for figures? These skills and hobbies can easily be turned into a business.

3. Is there something someone else is doing that I can do better myself?

If you've bought something and been unimpressed, why not step in, set up a business, and provide a better offer? Many good ideas stem from spotting products and services that can simply be improved upon or offered for less.

* * *

Your idea will develop over time. Don't be surprised if in 12 months' time it looks different to when you started out. This is okay. Business ideas tend to get refined over time; your offer will get sharper the more experience you gain in the marketplace. What's important is to get started with the beginnings of an idea – there'll be time to develop it as you get feedback from customers and input from others.

CASE STUDY

NAME: Katie Smith | BUSINESS: Tastes Marvellous

Having watched her mum successfully grow her own kitchen supplies business, Katie Smith had a good grounding in the ins and outs of running a start-up. It also helped her find the gap in the market for her start-up, Tastes Marvellous, founded when she was 18.

"Tastes Marvellous came about when a customer in Thailand bought a cake tin from my mum's business," explains Katie. "She asked us if there was any chance we could nip to Tesco and pop some Bisto in her order. I thought that if this one lady needed a service like that then there had to be other potential customers out there looking for the same kind of thing."

So Katie founded Tastes Marvellous, selling 'food from home' to expats across the world. She supplies British favourites to those living in markets where they're unavailable, doing a mean line in everything from Bisto to Marmite. "Once I got started," says Katie, "it grew quickly; and sales are still increasing."

Katie promotes the site through Google AdWords and expat blogs and websites.

"I would like to crack Japan and the Middle East," she says. "I am currently talking to the Japanese Embassy. I'm also signed up for a year-long programme with UK Trade & Investment, which should give me access to good information and contacts."

She's even started a second venture, Kate & Sydney, to take advantage of the overseas popularity of British products shown by the success of Tastes Marvellous. Kate & Sydney offers a range of bags decorated with cockney rhyming slang – quintessentially British and likely to be popular with the Olympics and Diamond Jubilee in 2012.

"I know from watching my mum's business that you usually don't finish up where you begin," says Katie. So she's aiming high. Her ambition is to keep Tastes Marvellous growing and to see her bags "in a department store by the end of 2012". We wouldn't bet against her.

* **www.tastesmarvellous.co.uk**

TOP TIP: "There's no such thing as not being able to do something ... If you think it's a good idea, just do it! The motto my mum swears by is, 'Say yes to everything and worry about the detail afterwards'. So far, that motto has not let me down!"

50 ideas for businesses

These are all ideas and businesses we have seen and profiled on Enterprise Nation. Many of them started as '5 to 9' businesses. In other words, a business started whilst the entrepreneur was in full-time study or employment. Find out more about this on page 55.

Blogger
Vlogger
Social media advisor
eBay trader
Online store owner
Giftware maker
Giftware seller
Artisan
Cupcake maker
Cosmetics producer
Hair and make-up artist
Origami artist
Picture artist
Furniture marker
Jewellery designer
Footwear designer
Fashion designer

Clothing producer
Toymaker
Party organiser
DJ
Musician
Magician
Beer producer
Events organiser
Wedding planner
Mystery shopper
Image consultant
Fitness advisor
Personal trainer
Photographer
Accountant
Lawyer

Translator
IT services
App developer
Software developer
Print and web designer
Network marketer
Pet care
Product manufacturer
E-learning provider
Facebook developer
Magazine publisher
T-shirt maker
Papercrafter
Dance instructor
Perfumer
Balloon decorator
Street advertiser

There are so many possibilities. You might even have too many ideas. In which case, don't be afraid to spend some time on all of them and, wherever possible, let the customer decide – try them out in small ways and see what gets the warmest response.

Niche is nice

When coming up with your idea, bear in mind that *niche* businesses are often ideal. Meeting the needs of a very well-defined audience helps keep your efforts focused and your offering clear in a crowded market. It also means success should naturally consolidate itself. So rather than just blogging, it's better to set up a blog focused on helping businesses make the most of Facebook (p.83). Rather than selling shoes, it's better to sell shoes specifically for people with big feet (p.162)

With a niche business:

- **you keep marketing costs low**, as your audience is well-defined; you know where your audience are and understand the kind of marketing messages to which they will respond

- **customer loyalty remains high**, as you become the expert in your field or the only provider of certain products; customers will want to stay with you and benefit from the specialist product or service you offer.

> **FRIENDS AND FAMILY FOCUS GROUP:** Talk to family and friends and ask them where they think your talents lie. They might just help you discover your business idea in an area you hadn't thought of.

The niche list

Here are some businesses I've come across that have benefited from having a clear niche. A few of them are profiled in this guide:

- Collie Wobbles (www.colliewobbles.co.uk) | *Border Collie/sheepdog-related products*

- Rock 'n' Roll Bride (www.rocknrollbride.com) | *For brides wanting a rock 'n' roll wedding*

- WorkSnug (www.worksnug.com) | *For mobile workers seeking connected spaces*

- Large Cup Lingerie (www.largecuplingerie.com) | *A shop dedicated to large cup bras and lingerie*
- Pai Skincare (www.paiskincare.com) | *Organic skincare for people with sensitive skin*
- Petite Cake Balls (facebook.com/PetiteCakeBalls) | *Bite-sized cakes*
- Tastes Marvellous (www.tastesmarvellous.co.uk) | *Sells British food products to expats around the globe*
- Yang Li Feng (www.yanglifeng.com) | *Sources high-end luxury products for the Chinese market*

* * *

Whatever the idea, good ones tend be based on what you enjoy, what people will buy and something that improves on what's already available. Think about how you can fashion your idea so it has a clear purpose for a clearly defined audience.

Use this template to help come up with your idea:

Template 1: What's the Big Idea?

Have I spotted a gap in the market?

What is my passion/hobby/skill?

Is there something I've seen that I can do better myself?

What about buying into someone else's idea via a franchise?

An idea as part of the package

If you're not able to settle on a viable idea of your own, consider using your StartUp Loan to buy into someone else's idea. You can do so through a franchise or signing up as a party-plan consultant and/or direct sales agent. Benefit from being your own boss whilst having the support of a central team and the proven idea that comes with it!

Here are 20 top franchise or party-plan opportunities (from *50 Fantastic Franchises!*, Brightword Publishing, 2011).

- My Secret Kitchen | www.mysecretkitchen.co.uk
- Jamie at Home | www.jamieathome.com
- The Pampered Chef | www.pamperedchef.co.uk
- Girlie Gardening | www.girliegardening.com
- Avon | www.avon.uk.com
- Kleeneze | www.kleeneze.com
- Neal's Yard | www.nealsyardremedies.com
- Maid2Clean | www.maid2clean.co.uk
- Razzamataz | www.razzamataz.co.uk

- Harmony At Home | www.harmonyathome.co.uk
- Shoes Glorious Shoes | www.shoesgloriousshoes.co.uk
- Travel Counsellors | www.travelcounsellors.co.uk
- Tatty Bumpkin | www.tattybumpkin.com
- Barrett & Coe | www.barrettandcoe.co.uk
- Barking Mad | www.barkingmad.uk.com
- Curves | www.curves.co.uk
- Spanish Amigos www.spanishamigos.co.uk
- ChipsAway | www.chipsaway.co.uk
- Usborne Books | www.usborne.com
- Captain Tortue Group | www.captaintortuegroup.com

USEFUL LINKS

- Direct Selling Association | www.dsa.org.uk
- British Franchise Association | www.thebfa.org
- *50 Fantastic Franchises!* eBook | www.brightwordpublishing.com

CASE STUDY

NAME: **Lauren Moulsley** | **BUSINESS:** **Avon (direct selling)**

After completing her A-levels, 19-year old Lauren Moulsley saw setting up her own business as an effective way of developing her business skills and getting her career started whilst at university. So Lauren, who started at Bournemouth University in September 2010, sells Avon products to friends and fellow students in halls.

"I enjoy being able to run my own business whilst at university," she says. "That and the fact I can supplement my student loan." Her Avon enterprise is currently a part-time commitment that she fits around her studies. Lauren feels she is setting herself up a good foundation in business, one which she can build on after graduation.

"With increasing competition for graduate vacancies, I saw business ownership as a serious choice for my future. It's great to have an income that's independent of the crowded graduate job market."

● **www.avon.uk.com** | @avon_uk

CASE STUDY

NAME: Richard Brigg | **BUSINESS: Usborne Books (direct selling)**

Richard Brigg is 24, works a job in sales by day and in his spare time develops his Usborne direct-selling business in the North of England, where he sees an opportunity to build a significant business. With Usborne, he gets the flexibility and training to make this a reality.

"I became an Usborne seller 12 months ago as I wanted to work around my day job and develop a business in my spare time.

"Usborne was Children's Publisher of the Year, 2012. As I did a journalism degree and have family members who teach, I've always been interested in reading and surrounded by books. So you could say this was the ideal business opportunity.

"I'm based in West Yorkshire and with Usborne being so strong in the South, I see great potential to expand the business across the North. I sell books at events such as home parties and I'm looking to develop more activity with local schools."

When it comes to receiving support for growing the business, where does Richard turn?

"I turn to the company intranet where Usborne sellers give each other a lot of help and I take inspiration from Emma Butt who is a highly successful Usborne seller and my division head."

Usborne may be a part-time venture for Richard at this point but if he reaches his goals, this situation will change.

"Goal number one for me is to earn as much from Usborne as I'm earning from my day job. Then I'd like to encourage more men to join Usborne. There's an incredible business opportunity with this network and I'm keen to tell as many people as possible about it!"

● **www.usborne.com** | **www.mylittleyellowduck.co.uk** | @Usborne

" Choose a business idea that you are passionate about. You're going to be spending a lot of time on it. And when you're working on something you love, it stops being work and feels more like fun. "

– Michael Acton-Smith,
founder, Moshi Monsters

2. RESEARCH THE MARKET

You have your idea. Turning it into a business requires some research, followed by a straightforward exercise in building that research into a plan. Here's how to go about it.

First, **research your potential customers**, the competition and a price point by visiting competitors' sites, online trade sites/forums, reading reports, and seeking intelligence from experts.

Look for data and comments that will answer the following questions:

- What is the number of potential customers you can serve, and how do these customers like to be served?
- What are their core characteristics and spending patterns, and who are their key influences?
- Who is currently serving your market?
- Where are your potential customers going for their goods and services?
- What do they like about what they're getting and, more importantly, what do they dislike (as this opens up opportunities for you to improve on the status quo)?

In view of the above, what price can you charge for your product/service?

Price yourself at a rate that's competitive with other providers in the market, that takes into account the amount of time, personal service and added value you offer, and that will turn a profit at the end of the day.

WHAT AM I WORTH? How much do you think customers or clients would pay for your product or service? Take a look at how similar offerings are priced and talk to people about how much they'd be willing to pay. Then talk to suppliers to check you can source materials and deliver at a price that covers your costs. Since starting a business from home (which we recommend you do!) will save you lots of money, you can pass some of these savings onto your customers. It will give you an edge over other businesses. But don't undercharge for the expertise and knowledge you offer. Only consider charging less for work that will reflect well on your business and boost your reputation, perhaps in the media or with a particularly impressive customer.

You can also source primary, or firsthand, data by conducting a survey or posing questions on social media channels.

Survey tools

- SurveyMonkey | www.surveymonkey.com
- Wufoo | www.wufoo.com

Social media channels

- Twitter | www.twitter.com
- Facebook | www.facebook.com
- LinkedIn | www.linkedin.com

Or, of course, you can hit the streets with a clipboard!

It was an unpleasant experience in a department store that highlighted a gap in the market for Cha Haxell (p.15). And it was talking to friends and family that provided the research she needed to launch her niche lingerie business.

Work on your own market research plan by completing the template on pages 16–17.

The name game

Coming up with an idea and carrying out research will get you thinking about what to name your business. If selling your knowledge, the company could be named after you – for example, 'Emma Jones Advisory Services'. In which case, job done! But if you're looking for something else, think of a name that:

- is easy to spell
- has an available domain name
- is not already registered with Companies House (use the free web-check service to access existing company names at www.companieshouse.gov.uk)
- people will remember.

You might want to protect the name with a trademark. See page 35 for information on how to go about that.

If you get stuck, visit Enterprise Nation (www.enterprisenation.com) where you will find people who can help you: the site is buzzing with talented copywriters and wordsmiths. Also, be sure to visit the 'Name your Business' section on Business Link for more guidance: tinyurl.com/nameyourbusiness

CASE STUDY

NAME: **Cha Haxell** | BUSINESS: **Large Cup Lingerie**

Cha Haxell was 24 and planning to take a master's degree in sports science when a bad experience in a high street store and a glance at some unflattering photos of herself led her down a different path, and into running a business with a very particular niche.

"I went into a store that's quite well-known for bra fittings and when I told them I wanted a 30-inch back, they told me to check the children's department. The effect that could have on the confidence of someone younger could be really detrimental. It made me want to help people find bras that fitted.

"I already knew my size because I'd had a proper fitting after looking at some pictures of myself on my birthday. An ill-fitting bra makes you look fatter than you are because you don't have a properly defined shape, and I thought I looked horrendous. At the same time, if the back's too big it's not giving you the proper support, which can be physically damaging. I spoke to friends and lots of them have small backs, too, but were wearing the wrong size bra.

"So I started contacting suppliers with a view to starting a business that sold better-fitting bras. The suppliers told me I needed to show them I was serious about selling their bras: I had to demonstrate my aims, how I was going to sell their products, and who else I was going to stock. I got the bones of a website together, got in touch again and said: 'This is what I'm going to do'."

Tapping into an international niche

Cha focused initially on the UK market, but then started targeting the international market. "Poor bra sizing is an international problem, and I was already making some overseas sales," she explains. Thanks to free international delivery she now makes "a lot of sales to the US, Canada and Australia." And whenever she goes on holiday, she checks out local stores. This, and a flourishing blogging community around the world, helps her keep tabs on market developments. "I do a lot of social networking, too, especially through Facebook and Twitter."

Cha is quick to praise the services of "a great marketing company that has helped a lot":

"They told me that having an amazing website and not marketing it properly is like opening a lovely new shop in the middle of nowhere that no one knows about. So I'm always trying to engage customers. And I make a lot of decisions based on speaking to customers and feedback from social media. I've considered moving into hosiery, for example, but it's a matter of seeing what's popular. I want to make sure I'm giving people what they want."

- **www.largecuplingerie.com** | **www.facebook.com/largecupbras** | @LargeCupLingerie

Template 2: Market Research

How big is the market?

What is the number of potential customers I can serve and how do these customers like to be served?

What are their characteristics, spending patterns and who are their key influences?

Who is currently serving my market?

Where are my potential customers going for their goods and services?

What do they like about what they're getting, and, more importantly, what do they dislike?

What price can I charge for my product/service?

What's competitive and takes into account the amount of time, personal service and added value that I offer?

SWOT analysis

With your idea, and now your research in-hand that supports it, prepare a SWOT analysis. This stands for: **S**trengths, **W**eaknesses, **O**pportunities, **T**hreats and looks as follows:

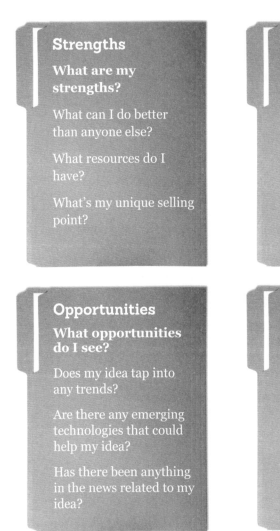

Strengths

What are my strengths?

What can I do better than anyone else?

What resources do I have?

What's my unique selling point?

Weaknesses

What are my weaknesses?

What should I avoid?

Where do I lack skills?

What might hinder my success?

Opportunities

What opportunities do I see?

Does my idea tap into any trends?

Are there any emerging technologies that could help my idea?

Has there been anything in the news related to my idea?

Threats

What threats might I face?

Who's my competition?

Does changing technology affect my idea?

Template 3: SWOT Analysis

Strengths

What are my strengths?

Weaknesses

What are my weaknesses?

Opportunities

What opportunities do I see?

Threats

What threats might I face?

3. WRITE A PLAN

A business plan will act as your map. It will guide the business from start to growth, with reference to milestones along the way.

The plan will include information about how you intend to get started and what your ultimate objectives are – and how you aim to get from one to the other. You might want to start a business and sell it in a few years' time, or grow to a point where you wouldn't want to grow anymore. And in between all that there will be significant steps to take.

Of course, you'll need to refer to resources: what you have already, what you'll need and how you'll pay for it.

So, after coming up with an idea and doing your research, writing the business plan is your first practical step to starting your business. With it under your belt you can say, "I'm off!"

Or IMOFF. It's an easy way to remember the headings to include in your business plan: **I**dea, **M**arket, **O**perations, **F**inancials and **F**riends. Have these as headings in your plan and you've taken a big step closer to becoming your own boss.

Idea

What's your idea?

Market

Who will be your customers or clients? And who is your competition?

Operations

How will you develop the idea, promote it and provide good customer service?

Financials

Can you earn more than you spend, so that the business makes a profit? Do you need any funds to get started?

Friends

Do you have a support network on hand for when you need business advice? Are there complementary businesses you've identified with whom partnerships are a possibility?

Return regularly to you plan to check progress against targets or to make amends as you respond to new opportunities.

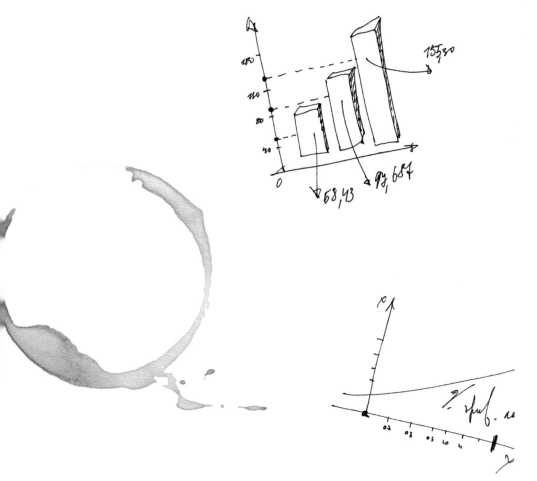

Executive Summary

Summarise what's in the rest of the plan. Something like this:

The vision for ABC is to become the leading company for selling xxx to xxx. This plan sets out how the vision will be achieved in the period 2012-2014. It outlines the product on offer, provides data on the market and shows how you will have the company operating profitably within the first three months.

Having identified a clear gap in the market, I'm excited about the opportunity to start and build a successful business that will offer a quality product [or service] to a well-defined market.

A. Person
Founder, Company ABC

The Idea

Include here your 'elevator pitch'; what is your product and how will it benefit the customer?

This is the opportunity to explain the idea of the business in a few sentences.

* This title would be more like 'Advisory Board' if preparing the plan for a bank or funder.

The Market

Customers

Who will be your customers? Include the quantity, their demographic profile, geographic locations, social backgrounds; essentially any strong data that shows you know your audience.

Competition

Who is selling a similar product/service? How do you differ from them? What is your unique selling point?

You can do this by producing a table that lists the competition. Outline what makes you stand out in the market: is it that your service will be online, that you'll charge a different price, have an innovative marketing approach or offer the service with a special extra twist?

Operations

The CEO

You have come up with the idea for the business and you've done your research on the market. Now it's time for the reader to know a bit about you! Note your background, skills, experience and any credentials for running this business. Plus information on other key members of staff (if there are any).

Sourcing

If this applies to your business, refer to how you'll source your product/service. You may be making it yourself!

Sales & Marketing

How will you promote what you offer to your customers? Include a brief sales and marketing plan with headings like this:

Press – how many press releases do you plan to distribute each year and to which press channels: newspapers, magazines, radio, etc.?

Online – will you have your own blog/website? Mention other sites that you'll approach for reciprocal links.

Partners – what about marketing tie-ups with other companies selling to the same audience?

You know where your customers are, so let your marketing plan show that you'll reach them in print, online and even in the streets!

Systems

You've sourced the service/product and told customers about it. Refer here to the process customers will go through to buy from you and the systems you'll have in place to deliver in time and on budget. Systems that may include online ordering and payment, a professional call-handling service to take orders or maybe some specific software.

Financials

Last but not least come the figures. Make this as clear as possible and it's probably best to do it in table form:

	Year 1	Year 2
Revenue		
Overheads		
Office rent		
Salary		
Stock		
Technology		
Marketing		
Travel & expenses		
Projected profit		

Drawing up a simple financial forecast will highlight any need to borrow money. The loan distribution agency you apply to will likely ask for this.

Friends & Family

In starting and growing your business, will you call on friends and family for advice? If so, refer to this here; mention your board of advisors, your experts-on-call, your support network!

(See page 158 onwards for details on how to access expert advisors and find a mentor whose details you can also include here.)

Template 4: Business Plan

Use this template to write your own business plan.

Executive Summary

The Idea

The Market

Customers

Competition

Operations

The CEO

Sourcing

Sales & Marketing

Press

Online

Partners

Systems

Friends & Family

Financials

" Avoid giving a personal guarantee – for a bank loan, property lease, whatever. There will always be another way. "

– Luke Johnson, founder, Risk Capital Partners

4. REGISTER THE COMPANY

When you set up in business, there are a couple of organisations you need to contact: Companies House and HM Revenue & Customs (HMRC). Before registering with either, have a think about the company status that suits you best.

Self-employed

This status means you are working for yourself. You keep records and accounts of your own activities and, in acting alone, get to keep all the profits – but are also solely liable for any debts.

Partnership

If you'd like to be self-employed but want to work with a friend or colleague, consider a partnership. It means that two or more people share the risks, costs and workload.

Zac Williams formed a partnership in a move that's helped the company grow. Read his story on page 28 and see pages 149–50 for details on how to form a partnership agreement.

Limited company

Limited companies exist in their own right, with the company's finances kept separate from the personal finances of its owners, so your liability is limited.

* * *

The status of your company will affect how much admin you have to do and the kind of financial records that you need to keep and file. Take advice from your accountant or local tax office on which one to choose.

CASE STUDY

NAME: **Zac Williams** | BUSINESS: **GradTouch**

Zac Williams, 23, set up GradTouch after graduating from the University of Durham with a degree in theology in 2010. A support service that 'bridges the gap' between graduates and employers, the business has grown rapidly and now employs 11 people.

"I started GradTouch in October 2010," says Zac, "but it began to get really serious when my business partner Joe Twigg came on board in April 2011. We started out giving students and graduates support with CVs and job applications and putting on events for employers on campus."

"We kind of stumbled into recruitment," says Zac. "We realised we had a good captive audience, so we created a free online platform that turns the traditional jobs board on its head." With GradTouch, if you're (for example) interested in marketing "you can read all about what it's like and where you can work, read company profiles and *then* see what jobs are available."

The company has grown quickly. "At first I was living at home in Manchester," says Zac, "and operating as a sole trader. My parents were very supportive and I had a couple of part-time jobs so it wasn't too much of a financial strain. When Joe came on board we incorporated and moved into a two-man office on a short lease and we've been getting bigger spaces as we've needed them."

The company now has five full-time employees, four part-timers (on freelance contracts), two interns and 42 'campus ambassadors' – "students who we employ," says Zac, "to help us with campus activities. Employing people just came quite naturally. We needed them so we took them on."

Growing the business

"Joe and I both put in a small amount of money," says Zac, "but we've been relying on what we've been making to grow further. We've been lucky to get people on board who have helped us grow, so we're looking at the possibility of giving our employees shares to supplement their pay – it makes people more committed to the business if they have something invested in it."

When it comes to expansion, GradTouch is "never happy staying still". Explains Zac: "Though we have a business plan, it keeps changing because we try to be as flexible as possible."

www.gradtouch.com | www.facebook.com/gradtouch | @gradtouch

TOP TIP 1: "Get as much advice as possible from anyone you know who has anything to do with your area of business. I speak to a lot of people who have been involved in graduate schemes and we get advice from our business clients, too. It's good to get as many viewpoints as possible."

TOP TIP 2: "It definitely helps to get an idea of what people need, because you can end up filling a hole that no one wants filling. But even if everyone had said, 'No, that's not a good idea', I would still have started GradTouch. Starting a business is not something to be feared. It's exciting."

Being social

Should you decide to start a social enterprise – a business trading for social and environmental purposes – there are additional legal structures to consider, including:

- community interest company (CIC)
- industrial and provident society
- charitable status.

To find out more about launching a social enterprise or creating a CIC visit:

- Social Enterprise UK | www.socialenterprise.org.uk
- CIC Regulator | www.cicregulator.gov.uk
- 'Thinking about starting a Social Enterprise?' via Business Link | tinyurl.com/startingasocialenterprise

Carly Ward set up Young Entrepreneur Society (www.youngentsoc.org.uk) when she was 19 as a company to teach young people enterprising skills. The venture was created as a social enterprise.

"As a social enterprise company, YES has social objectives and is not primarily driven by the need to maximise profits for the owners but to reinvest surpluses into the business or community. We will be investing in our young entrepreneurs and also giving grants in the near future."

Companies House

When registering with Companies House, there are three options from which to choose. You can buy a ready-made company from a company formation agent, incorporate a company yourself by sending documents and a registration fee to Companies House or register online via the Business Link service. If you decide to complete registration yourself, see form IN01 – application to register a company.

- **Business Link** | Incorporate online with Business Link (tinyurl.com/incorporateyourcompany) and pay £18.

- **Self-incorporation** | Visit the new company registration page of the Companies House website: bit.ly/dw1xcJ. Complete form IN01. Post to Companies House with relevant fee. Standard service fee of £40 (documents processed in eight to ten days). Same-day service fee is £100.

- **Company formation agent** | Visit websites such as Jordans (www.jordans.co.uk), Companies Made Simple (www.companiesmadesimple.com) and UK Plc (www.uk-plc.net). Prices start at £25/£30 for standard company registration.

HM Revenue & Customs

The rules on registering a new business with HM Revenue & Customs are pretty clear-cut. You are required to register as soon as you start earning from any business activity. As stated, you can choose to register as self-employed, as a partnership, or as a limited company. Each category has its own filing requirements, as shown below.

Sole trader/self-employed

The calculation of tax and National Insurance owing is done through self-assessment.

You either need to complete a form CWF1, or simply call the newly self-employed business helpline. It should be done by 5 October after the end of the tax year in which you started your business to avoid a fine.

- Form CWF1 | **www.hmrc.gov.uk/forms/cwf1.pdf**
- Helpline for the newly self-employed | 0845 915 4515

It's not onerous to complete the form and, once registered, you'll be classified as self-employed and sent a self-assessment tax return each year, which you complete, showing your income and expenses from self-employment as well as details of your employment elsewhere (if that applies).

You will be subject to tax and National Insurance on any profits you make, but the good news is that any losses incurred can be offset against your employed income (if you have any), which could even result in a tax rebate.

Depending on your turnover and how straightforward your tax affairs are, you may be able to simply fill out the short tax return (SA200). However, this cannot be self-selected, nor is it on the HMRC website or orderable; HMRC will send it to you automatically if they think you qualify, based on information given in the previous year's return. If you have turnover below £68,000, it's likely that you will qualify. As ever, though, it will depend on individual circumstances, and the law (and various criteria it uses) may change!

Deadlines

Self-assessment tax return deadlines are as follows:

- paper tax returns should be received by HMRC by 31 October
- online tax returns should be completed by 31 January (giving you an extra three months).

Useful links

- Leaflet SE1 – 'Thinking of working for yourself?' |
  www.hmrc.gov.uk/leaflets/se1.pdf

- Helping you understand self assessment and your tax return, HMRC |
  www.hmrc.gov.uk/sa

Partnership

According to HMRC, a partnership is where:

"Two or more people set up a business. Each partner is personally responsible for all the business debts, even if the debt was caused by another partner. As partners, each pays income tax on their share of the business profits through self-assessment, as well as National Insurance."

In terms of filing requirements, each partner should complete a partnership supplementary page as part of their individual self-assessment tax return. This is in addition to a partnership return, which has to be submitted by one nominated partner and show each partner's share of profits/losses.

Deadlines

The deadlines for partnership tax returns are as follows:

- paper tax returns should be received by HMRC by 31 October

- online tax returns should be completed by 31 January (giving you an extra three months).

Limited company

Limited companies exist in their own right, with the company's finances distinct from the personal finances of the owners. What this means is that the company is liable for any debts, not the individual owners, as is the case if you are self-employed or in a partnership.

In April 2008 it became legal to form and run a limited company with just one person, without the need to involve anyone else (prior to this you also needed a company secretary). As noted, you can form a new limited company by registering with Companies House (www.companieshouse.gov.uk), registering online via Business

Link (tinyurl.com/incorporateyourcompany) or by using a company creation agent.

As well as registering with Companies House, you also need to let HMRC know you are operating as a limited company. And you will need to set up and register a PAYE scheme, as you are an employee of the company.

- Register PAYE scheme | www.hmrc.gov.uk/newemployers

- New employer's helpline | 0845 60 70 143

In terms of filing requirements, you should complete a self-assessment company tax return at the end of the accounting period. The return will show the company's taxable profits and whether any corporation tax is owed, and can be filed online at www.hmrc.gov.uk/ct.

The return should also be filed with Companies House to comply with the Companies Act 2006. This can be done free of charge, using the online WebFiling service at Companies House: ewf.companieshouse.gov.uk.

On your returns, you can claim wear-and-tear allowances (capital allowances) on any equipment you buy, and an element of your expenses for working from home. You can also claim travelling expenses, subsistence and a proportion of your phone calls.

Deadlines

Whereas filing deadlines for self-assessment and partnership tax returns are specific dates, that is not the case with company tax returns, which must be filed 12 months after the end of your company's corporation tax accounting period.

IN GOOD ORDER: Keep records of your business dealings – this will make it much easier to complete tax returns when the time comes. Keep hold of **receipts** of business-related **purchases**; **copies of invoices** to customers; **bank statements**, especially if you don't yet have a separate account for the business (it is worth starting one); **utility bills** (if you are starting the business from home and using part of the house for business), which can be claimed as a business expense and so reduce your tax bill.

For advice from HMRC on good record keeping, visit:
www.hmrc.gov.uk/startingup/keeprecs.htm

VAT

Whichever company status you choose, if your business turns over more than £77,000 (in the 2012/13 tax year), or you think your turnover will soon exceed this amount, you should also register for value added tax (VAT).

You can voluntarily register at any time. Being VAT-registered can bring credibility with certain customers, but adding VAT to your invoices may make you more expensive than competitors and you will have to file a VAT return four times a year.

- 'How and when to register for VAT', HMRC |
  www.hmrc.gov.uk/vat/start/register

Accountant accompaniment

Talk to a qualified accountant about the structure that is best for your business. And consider employing their services to complete your tax returns. Even if your accounts are very simple, it is well worth seeking professional advice, particularly as the rules and regulations can change frequently and without warning.

Find an accountant by visiting:

- ICAEW [Institute of Chartered Accountants for England and Wales] |
  www.icaew.com
- Accountant partners of online software tool, FreeAgent |
  www.freeagent.com/partners

Useful links

- 'Starting a Business', HMRC | www.hmrc.gov.uk/startingup
- 'Tax Help – and advice for small business' | www.businesslink.gov.uk/taxhelp

5. PROTECT THE BRAND

You have now registered with Companies House and HM Revenue & Customs. Your final consideration should be your intellectual property. You may decide to register a trademark to protect your company name or brand or, if you've come up with a unique invention, a patent. Registering either means that companies can't come along and use your name or invention without your permission.

The four forms of IP

There are four different kinds of intellectual property that you can protect:

1. Patents

These protect, essentially, what makes things work. For example, says the Intellectual Property Office (IPO), "what makes a wheel turn or the chemical formula of your favourite fizzy drink".

2. Trademarks

These are "signs (like words and logos) that distinguish goods and services in the marketplace".

3. Designs

What a logo or product looks like: "from the shape of an aeroplane to a fashion item".

4. Copyright

An automatic right that comes into existence for anything written or recorded.

Register and protect your intellectual property by visiting the UK Intellectual Property Office website (www.ipo.gov.uk).

See page 145 to read the story of how Charlie Ashworth started life as a freelance toy inventor before becoming a qualified patent attorney and starting a business to help other small businesses take care of their intellectual property.

6. TAKE CARE OF HOUSEHOLD ADMIN

When starting out, you're likely be starting from home – your own, your parents' or at university. It's the best way to start, keeping costs low and commute short. In other words: more time and money for the business.

You'll probably be outsourcing work as opposed to employing staff, so there's no need for lots of people to come into the office each day. And you can meet clients and contacts in the local hotel or serviced work space. It's also good to know you're not alone in starting at home – over 60% of businesses do. You may have a few questions around household admin and who you need to tell. Here are the answers.

Q: Do I need planning permission?

A: You'll only need planning permission to base the business at home if you answer 'yes' to any of these questions:

- will your home no longer be used mainly as a private residence?
- will your business result in a marked rise in traffic or people calling?
- will your business involve any activities that are unusual in a residential area?
- will your business disturb the neighbours at unreasonable hours or create other forms of nuisance such as noise or smells?

If your house is pretty much going to remain a house, with your business quietly accommodated within it, then permission won't be required. If you're unsure, contact your local council to seek their views (www.planningportal.gov.uk).

Q: Do I need to tell the local authority I'm working from home?

A: Depends on whether you pass the planning test. If you need planning permission, you'll have to inform your local authority. If you don't, then the only benefit of telling them is that they'll charge you business rates (rather than council tax) on the part of the house being used for business purposes – not really much of an incentive! Business rates are different in each area and something that should be agreed with your local authority. Check out the Nusiness Link guide to business rates at bit.ly/hXHq6q.

Q: Do I need to tell the landlord?

A: Yes, it's best to let them know that you will be working from home. Good news is, the Housing Minister announced on 1 November 2010 that social landlords should review any contracts prohibiting people from working from home, making it much easier for people in social housing to use living space as work space. Since then we've seen some social landlords such as London & Quadrant (www.lqgroup.org.uk) organise business training for tenants. A welcome sight.

Q: What about my insurance provider? Do they need to know?

A: Yes, do inform your insurance company. Tell them about the equipment and stock you have at home. An upgrade from domestic to a business policy is not expensive so don't be put off in making this call. Your insurance provider is likely to recommend that you also take out public liability insurance in case anyone who comes to visit suffers an injury in or around your home office. See the next page for a guide to all kinds of insurance.

Q: Do I need protection for when customers and contacts come to visit?

A: Yes, carry out a health and safety check, which is easy to do by following the steps set out by the Health and Safety Executive (www.hse.gov.uk) in their *Homeworking* guide (available at bit.ly/aGDc8N).

Q: Should I tell the neighbours?

A: Yes. When working from home, it's worth keeping your neighbours firmly on side. You don't want them getting annoyed by any deliveries or distractions. If you know of a time when there'll be an unusual amount of activity in your home office, let your them know in advance and perhaps send a bottle of wine.

INSURANCE INS-AND-OUTS

There are different categories of insurance which you need to know about to secure the policy that's right for you. The main ones are:

1. **PROFESSIONAL INDEMNITY** – relevant to businesses offering services and knowledge. Provides protection if you receive a claim alleging a negligent act, error or omission committed by you in the course of the conduct of your professional business.

2. **PUBLIC LIABILITY** – advisable to have if clients are visiting your home office and/or you are supplying goods to consumers. This will protect you in the event of potential injury to business visitors and/or damages arising from the supply or sale of goods which have caused injury to a third party or their property.

3. **BUSINESS INTERRUPTION** – covers your potential loss of revenue following a material damage loss.

4. **EMPLOYER'S LIABILITY** – only applies when you have employees. Offers protection in the event of death or injury to them sustained in the course of their employment.

5. **MOTOR INSURANCE** – this is different to standard car insurance, which does not include business use. If you have a vehicle dedicated for business, you should buy motor insurance or get a business extension on your car insurance policy when using your existing car for business travel.

6. **HOME INSURANCE** – you are likely to already have a home insurance policy but this will generally not cover business activities carried out at home or business equipment within the home. Speak to your insurance provider and upgrade to a business policy. This is not usually costly but it will ensure you're protected.

Creating the perfect work environment

Wherever you've chosen to set up shop, create the perfect work environment by following this quick checklist to ensure you're working profitably and productively.

Find dedicated space

Try to create an area at home that functions as your dedicated workspace. That way you can better adjust into business mode. It's also useful for making clear to friends and family that when you're in your home office, you're working.

This dedicated space could be a spare room, in the attic, under the stairs, or even the garden shed.

Invest in a good desk and chair

You could be spending a good few hours each day at the desk and in your chair, so be sure they're both sturdy and comfortable. Buy a chair that's designed for computer use – and try it out first. The back experts say your feet should be flat on the floor and your back straight.

When it comes to computers, the top of your monitor or laptop screen should be at eye level and about an arm's length away from you. There are all sorts of docks that can help with this, but there's also no harm in using a sturdy pile of books and an external mouse/keyboard to achieve the same end.

Have a vision

Put a vision board up on the wall and stick pictures on it that represent your personal and business ambitions: places you want to visit, targets for the company, and people you enjoy spending time with. Glance at it each day. Remind yourself of everything you're working for.

Roam free

Install Wi-Fi so it's possible to work from anywhere on the property. To get started you need a wireless router. You may have received one free from your internet service provider. If not, check out respectable suppliers such as Netgear (www.netgear.co.uk). See 'Getting connected' on page 51 if you need support.

Support on tap

And finally, surround yourself with supporters. Friends or family, peers in online forums, contacts met at events; they can all help when it comes to celebrating your success or raising your spirits on a day that doesn't quite go as planned.

On pages 156–9 we cover where to go to find support and access mentors. For Oliver Sidwell, support was close to home when he started his business, RateMyPlacement:

"When we launched RateMyPlacement, my two co-founders and I worked from separate home offices. Mine happened to be my old bedroom back in the family home. I graduated from Loughborough University where the business had started, moved back in with my folks and the business of building the company started from there.

"As my dad also ran his business from home we often met in the kitchen at lunchtime and I shared progress from the day. Dad offered advice and guidance which, in the early stages, proved invaluable. I'm now living in London and the company is 20 people strong but I still hark back to those early days of sage advice, mum's welcome cups of tea and a top-notch laundry service!"

Leaving home

If an external office is right for you from the start, visit sites such as www.startupbritain.org/spaces to find available space in enterprise hubs, co-working spaces, government buildings and serviced offices. All needs and budgets catered for! See page 161 for details on 'accelerators', that come complete with space as part of the package.

IN THE KIT

Get one month's free virtual office or one month free in any Bizspace unit.

Get a value business start-up package from Regus, including impressive business address, call answering, mail-handling, business mentoring, drop-in business lounges and more.

For Katie Leamon, home was the start she needed, but moving into a studio has given her the support community and space to grow ...

CASE STUDY

NAME: **Katie Leamon** | BUSINESS: **Katie Leamon**

Katie Leamon describes herself as "a surface designer and illustrator with a passion for all things quaint." She always knew she would become her own boss. She just thought it would would be some time in the distant future – not soon after graduation.

First, though, Katie went to work for a women's clothing brand. A small company, she was able to learn about numerous business areas. "It taught me what I would and wouldn't do differently if I had my own company," says Katie. "The experience was invaluable."

Feeling it was time to do her own thing in 2010, Katie then began her own design business, staying in her day job but focusing on the new company at night and weekends. This helped her feel her way into the new business.

"I set up a desk in our communal lounge with the support of my housemates and started developing my designs and working on my website. That lasted until February."

At this point, her brother gave her the push she needed to give up her job. "I went full time in the business and shared a studio with him." That studio space is Make Space Studios (www.makespacestudios.com), a community of creatives including artists, graphic designers, illustrators and animators who work alongside each other and benefit from peer support.

Katie is promoting the business through Facebook and Twitter. She has a shop on Notonthehighstreet, as well as her own web store. She has also exhibited at a number of trade fairs, and has products stocked in Liberty and Paperchase in the UK. She's going global this year by launching in a department store in Switzerland and a boutique in Milan.

- www.katieleamon.com | @katieleamon

TOP TIP: "Spend some time working in and learning about your market before you start a business. If you're unsure of what way to start, just start: things have a habit of dictating their own path. Believe in yourself and your ideas, remember to take a step back sometimes and look at what you've achieved, without becoming complacent."

7. YOUR TECH SETUP

Putting together a tech setup for your new business needn't mean starting from scratch or spending lots of money. Once your business starts to grow, you can upgrade your tech as and when money becomes available.

To start with, there are affordable and free solutions that can get you up and running in no time at all. Chances are, you have some of them already.

So, let's take a look at what you might already have and what you might need to buy. We'll separate them by hardware and software.

Hardware

Computer

When starting out, using a shared computer will be just fine. Bear in mind, however, that in the first few months of starting your business, you may find yourself working more hours than usual trying to put it all together. So let your friends and family know you may be hogging the computer!

Also, when your business starts to grow, the information you collect – info on your customers, clients and contacts; including financial details – will become more and more valuable. You might then start to think twice about sharing your computer with other people.

You may already have your own laptop. If you don't, when you've got a bit of money behind you, look into buying one for your new business. Budget laptops start at around £300, but when buying a computer it sometimes pays to buy the best you can afford in order to prepare for the future.

IN THE KIT

Get £25 off any Vostro laptop or desktop worth over £400 with Dell.

Get a 10% discount on the HP ProBook 4540s Notebook with HP.

Processor

The processor is the speed of your computer. The higher the number, the faster your computer can run.

Memory

More memory (RAM) improves performance and enables your computer to run more programs at once. A common frustration amongst computer users is how long it can take to launch programs and switch between them. More RAM equals less waiting.

Hard drive

The hard drive gives you space for data and programs. This can easily be expanded with an additional, external, hard drive. You may be surprised at how quickly it will fill up, if your laptop is your only computer and you're also storing personal data, like music and photos, on it.

Peripherals

Multifunction printer

Even though I find myself using it less these days, I still think it's too early to pronounce the printer dead, especially if you use a multifunction printer like I do.

It's a real space-saver – imagine keeping a printer, scanner, photocopier and fax machine in one office. Mine sits neatly on my desk and is handy when I want to email sketches to my designer. He uses his to archive printed documents. When he receives important letters, for example, he scans them into his computer and recycles the hard copy! We're both on our way to paperless home offices.

External hard drive

External hard drives are great for adding more storage capacity to your computer but they're especially useful for backing up your machine. This is an important process, which you should do regularly – imagine what would happen if your computer crashed and wouldn't restart, or if it was dropped or stolen.

Macs have backing-up software built-in; as do the latest PCs. If not, try SuperDuper! for the Mac and True Image for the PC.

- SuperDuper! | www.shirt-pocket.com/SuperDuper
- True Image | www.acronis.com

Keyboard and mouse

If you're going to use a laptop, you probably won't get an additional keyboard and mouse. But you should think about it. Lots of time hunched over your laptop screen is no good for your neck and back. With an additional keyboard and mouse, and a stand that raises your laptop to eye-level, you can prevent a lifetime of aches and pains.

Some companies produce keyboards/mice which are ergonomically designed to prevent repetitive strain injury (RSI).

VoIP phones

You can make serious savings on your phone bill by using a VoIP phone. VoIP stands for 'voice over internet protocol' and basically means making calls over the internet rather than your phone line. As such, it's a much cheaper way of making calls (it's sometimes free). And it's the easiest way to set up a second line. The VoIP phone I use is made by a company called IPEVO.

- IPEVO | www.ipevo.com

Software

You may already be using many of these programs, so there's no need to splash out when setting up your business. Once it grows you can upgrade to more advanced versions if required. To start, here are the basics. Later we'll look at software (much of it free or very affordable) for when your business is up and running.

Office software

The industry standard in office software is Microsoft Office. If you're trying to save money, try these free alternatives:

- OpenOffice.org | www.openoffice.org
- Google Docs | www.google.com/docs

Both do pretty much everything that Microsoft Office does, and can open and save Microsoft Office files as well.

Web browser

Internet Explorer and Safari both do a good job when it comes to web browsing, as does Firefox. But there's a browser I use that I think is better. It's called Google Chrome and it's faster, more secure and more customisable.

You can add features that will help you do your work and manage your lifestyle. These include features to control your music (without having to switch programs), comparison shop and even change the way your browser looks. It's a free, small download, and it works on Macs and PCs. Its speedy and uncluttered nature makes it particularly good for netbook use.

- Google Chrome | www.google.com/chrome

Email

If you've got Microsoft Office you might use Outlook (or Entourage, as it's called in the Mac version), which is Outlook Express's big sister. It includes calendar and address book features, but it's not free (or cheap). On Macs, Mail is standard.

An alternative is provided by the people who make the Firefox browser. It's called Thunderbird and can do pretty much everything that Outlook can. You can also use it with web-based mail, like Gmail.

- Thunderbird | www.getthunderbird.com

SIGNATURE TOUCH: Make the most of the opportunity every time you click 'send' on an email. Include a professional email signature or sign-off that has your basic contact details (company name, website, postal address, telephone, etc.). And consider including a discreet mention of any seasonal or product offers, and your social media sites.

Instant messaging and VoIP

Lots of instant messaging programs also allow you to make video and voice calls. Skype integrates text, voice and video chat. With it you can make free calls to other Skype users and to landline or mobile phones for a small fee, deducted from pay-as-you-go style Skype credit.

You can assign a landline-esque phone number to your Skype account in order to receive calls at your computer, using a VoIP handset, or divert calls to your mobile when out and about.

- Skype | www.skype.com

Support

If you're in need of assistance with anything from hardware set-up to software installation, call in the help of a local IT expert. You may know a neighbour who's a dab hand at technology. If not, you can check out one of a growing number of companies who send a 'geek' direct to your door.

- Geeks-on-Wheels | www.geeks-on-wheels.com
- KnowHow | www.knowhow.com
- The Geek Squad | www.geeksquad.co.uk

On the move

Now that you've found the right technology for your office it's time to take it outside. If you ever get tired of your four walls, it's good to know that it's possible to work elsewhere. With a few simple tips and tricks you can enjoy total flexibility, and work from almost anywhere.

With your computer

If you have a laptop, you pretty much have all you need to work on the move. Almost all laptops come with built-in wireless receivers, so you can hop onto Wi-Fi in public places like coffee shops and libraries. But if you're not sure whether there'll be ample power supply where you're going, a spare battery is well worth considering.

SHOULD I BUY A TABLET COMPUTER OR A LAPTOP?

Like the rest of the world, you've probably been tempted by gorgeous tablet computers like Apple's iPad. But should you buy one instead of a laptop? Can you really get as much business-work done on a tablet?

Well, it really depends on the nature of your business. If you'll be out and about a lot, visiting clients and customers, then buying a tablet becomes a serious consideration. But if your work will involve lots of sitting at a desk or writing long documents, you may find that a tablet PC is not for you. The iPad is constantly improving as a business machine thanks to the App Store, but it still needs an external keyboard to cope with long writing sessions.

The future of computing could lie somewhere between tablets and laptops: ultrabooks. Ultrabooks are really thin, fast laptops. They have traditional features, like a full-size keyboard and trackpad, but usually no DVD drive and limited hard drive storage. That's okay though, as a lot of your work will take place in the 'Cloud' (more on that later!). Because of their size and weight, ultrabooks are really portable.

Technology has enabled David Young to run his international business from anywhere and alongside a full-time day job. He sees a future where everyone else will be doing the same. Why do people still need a permanent office, he asks?

CASE STUDY

NAME: **David Young** | BUSINESS: **Yang Li Feng**

David Young started Yang Li Feng in mid-2011 at the age of 25 and runs it flexibly around his full-time job. The company procures exclusive products for wealthy Chinese customers and offers a translation service and consultancy to British firms wanting to improve their approach to doing business with China.

Two experiences lie behind this successful start-up.

"The first is that I took a gap year in China before going to university," says David, "and found I was really out of my comfort zone. We'd go to a restaurant and couldn't order. We ended up showing people photographs of what we wanted; that's how I learnt the language."

"Secondly, after university I worked for an events company and realised we were doing business with the Chinese in a very westernised way and not taking our audience into account."

On top of this, David grew up near Bicester – "one of the top tourist destinations for Chinese visitors to the UK" – and realised "these guys were prepared to spend a lot of money buying exclusive products".

It all came together with Yang Li Feng. About 70% of the company's business is sourcing and buying products for Chinese customers, "often something that no one else has". David finds that "older customers want brands; younger ones will tend to say 'I saw this amazing product video on YouTube and I want something similar'. We find it for them."

"My partner's a professional translator, so we have a website translation service as well. And because I know what it's like to do business in China, we brief British business people on how to interact with Chinese delegates and business people. We work with a lot of antiques companies and luxury brands."

Running a flexible business

"I still work full-time," says David. This sees him getting up early to work "from 6-9" on the business, as well as in the evenings and at weekends. "I do everything via smartphones and tablets and we use Skype a lot. I don't need an office and it keeps my costs low."

"Technology has made my life so much easier," he continues. "I don't understand why the majority of businesses still have offices. My team can be based anywhere. My Shanghai operation is outsourced to a good friend, for example, and I'd like to work from Beijing in the future with someone looking after things here."

David currently has a team of four people to 'in-source' to: self-employed contractors that work within his business, as well as a few others for outsourcing. "Most of them I have found through LinkedIn. They let me know when they're free and they take a split of the income from the work they do.

"My feeling is that if you can have a secondary income that's £5,000 a year, that's better than saying 'I want to be a millionaire'. Start small and make it happen. You never know who's going to be in the audience."

●   **www.yanglifeng.com | www.linkedin.com/in/davidalyoung**

Getting connected

You'll need broadband right from the start: during your research, while you're setting up your business, through to when it grows and takes over the world!

Your two main options are ADSL broadband, which is offered by companies like BT, Orange and Sky, and cable broadband from Virgin Media. The biggest difference is that ADSL requires a phone line, while cable broadband does not.

The advantage of cable broadband is that if you don't have a landline phone, and always use your mobile, you can save money by not having to pay line rental on your phone as well as on your internet connection. It's often faster, too, but you'll need to check whether it's available in your area. ADSL broadband is more commonplace and there are lots of companies offering it. As always, read the fine print before you sign anything. Here are some things to look out for:

Price

Some broadband prices seem really cheap but often the prices advertised are for the first few months of an 18-month contract, so make sure you know what you're getting into.

Usage

Some broadband companies will set restrictions on the amount of data you can download in a month and sometimes even charge you extra if you go over your agreed limit. These limits rarely affect most users, but if your business is the kind that needs to send and receive lots of information, look for deals with generous monthly download allowances. Or, better still, unlimited downloads.

Customer support

If you're installing broadband for the first time, you might need some help setting up and, once you're up and running, for what to do when your connection suddenly drops. For these sorts of queries it's handy to have good customer support, so check to see what's on offer and, crucially, how much it should cost to call for help.

Network

Setting up a network used to be the work of professionals and, I suppose, in big companies it still is. But setting one up for your home by yourself is much easier these days.

There are two types of wireless router: one for ADSL internet service providers, like Sky and BT, and another for cable internet, like Virgin Media. Check with your internet service provider to find out which is the best router for your type of connection.

If you didn't get a router from your provider, check out Netgear.

- Netgear | **www.netgear.co.uk**

The Cloud

If you already use web mail, you'll be accustomed to the idea of your messages and contacts being available from any computer or device connected to the internet. So, how about running your entire business from any computer or device anywhere?

The Cloud refers to web apps. You run them through your web browser and all the data is stored online, so in effect you can use them from pretty much any computer anywhere!

The best example is provided by Google, whose Google Apps (www.google.com/a) offering includes email, instant messaging, a calendar, word processor, spreadsheet and presentation software, as well as a website builder. It's free and easy to use.

All the work you do is stored in 'The Cloud' so you can log in and out from anywhere and see the same information. Also, if your computer crashes or you buy a new system you won't lose any data or have to reinstall it on a new machine.

TEN FREE CLOUD APPS FOR YOUR BUSINESS

Cloud apps are not only fantastically useful, they don't take up room on your computer and you don't have to worry about backing up your data. They're also, more often than not, free to use.

Here are ten of our favourite free cloud apps for business.

1. Dropbox (**www.dropbox.com**) | Dropbox is like a thumb drive in the sky. It's a folder that sits on your computer, but its contents are stored remotely and synced across other computers and devices that are signed into your Dropbox account. No-nonsense sharing, if you're working with others, and peace of mind that your work is all backed up.

2. Evernote (**www.evernote.com**) | Evernote is a bit like Dropbox, but for your brain. It helps you "remember everything" by allowing you to capture notes and ideas, photos and screen grabs, sounds and links, sync them automatically to the cloud and access them from practically anywhere – great for the planning stages of your business.

3. Google Docs (**docs.google.com**) | As broadband gets quicker and more reliable, Google Docs is becoming a bit of a threat to Microsoft Office: it includes apps for word processing, spreadsheets, presentations, drawings and forms – except all the apps run inside your browser, rather than on your desktop. All of your work is stored in the cloud and it's super easy to collaborate with others in real time on the same document.

4. Gmail and Google Calendar (**mail.google.com**, **calendar.google.com**) | We've mentioned Gmail before, but did you know Google also made excellent calendar software? Both are really useful if you plan to work on the move.

5. Google Analytics (**www.google.com/analytics**) | When your website is up and running, you'll want to know how many people are visiting. Google Analytics, like most of Google's services, is free, and helps you understand your website statistics, including where your visitors are from, which pages they visited the most, and how they found your website in the first place.

6. HootSuite (**www.hootsuite.com**) | If social media is part of your marketing plan – and it probably is! – there's no better way to manage your social media presence than with HootSuite. It keeps you on top of your Twitter, Facebook and LinkedIn accounts, as well as what your customers and potential customers are saying about your business.

7. Delicious (**www.delicious.com**) | Delicious is a bookmarking service that keeps all of your important links in the cloud so you can get to them from any computer.

8. Toodledo (**www.toodledo.com**) | There's so much to do when starting a business, but you can keep on top of all your tasks with this free app. Get tasks out of your inbox by forwarding them to your Toodledo email address, organise them by folders, tags, context and subtasks, and sync them with your smartphone.

9. Basecamp (**www.basecamp.com**) | If some tasks involve other people and form part of larger projects, check out project management software, Basecamp. It allows you to share files, deliver projects on time and keep communication organised and out of your inbox.

10. MailChimp (**www.mailchimp.com**) | To make sure your business message is in other people's inboxes, put together a newsletter with MailChimp, send it out to your customer mailing list and track its success. Just make sure people have signed up to your mailing list before hitting 'send'!

8. WORKING 5 TO 9

You don't need to give up your studies or throw in the day job to get all this done. Nor do you need to for the next two stages – launch and growth. You can plan the business, register the business and continue to run the business successfully by 'working 5 to 9' – this is the term I apply to the five-million-plus people in the UK who are working or studying by day and building a business at night and weekends.

It's a sensible way to start and grow. If you're working a day job, you give yourself the time to build confidence and cash flow in the business, and can keep putting money aside until you're ready to go full time in your own venture.

Here's what you need to do regarding your current job and boss in order to make this as smooth as possible.

The contract

If you have written terms and conditions of employment they are likely to contain reference to the pursuit of personal business ventures outside your contracted working hours. The clauses to look out for include 'the employee's duties and obligations' and what is commonly known as 'whole time and effort'. These clauses require the employee to devote the whole of their time, attention and abilities to the business of the employer.

If your contract contains these or similar clauses, don't despair, as it doesn't necessarily mean you can't pursue your business. Many employment contracts are drafted using standard templates with little consideration to personal circumstance. You know your job better than anyone, so if you don't think your business venture will affect the way you do your job, it probably won't – and your employer will recognise this. Having checked how things stand in the contract, it's time to talk things through with your boss.

The conversation

Treat it as an amicable and informal conversation to gauge your employer's initial reaction.

I asked Patrick Lockton, a qualified lawyer, for his take on the matter and advice on how employees should go about having this conversation:

"When you approach your employer, be prepared to negotiate, be flexible and compromise. If you think it appropriate, make it clear your business venture will in no shape or form affect your ability to do your job or affect your employer's interests. If anything, it will make you a better, more confident and experienced employee and it will not cost your employer a thing."

Patrick goes on to say:

"After having such a conversation, you can do one of two things:

1. if your employer has not expressed any concerns about your intentions and you have no concerns of your own, disclose your intentions to your employer anyway. Treat it as something you want to do for the sake of clarity and for the record, as opposed to something you want their permission for; or

2. if your employer has expressed concerns, try and negotiate a package that you are both happy with. Address their concerns, agree some ground rules and get their permission in writing. Give your employer as much helpful information as possible. If you are going to need some time off or to change your hours then this is the time to bring it up.

"Always take written notes so that you don't forget what was said and so you can remind your employer what was agreed."

So long as you're not competing with your employer or breaching their trust, you shouldn't have any problem at all in pursuing your 5 to 9 ambitions. After all, as Patrick says, your employer benefits from all the new skills you're picking up, and it doesn't cost them a penny in training or resources!

Richard Hewitt is making the most of his employment to pick up the skills and experience that will stand him in good stead for his years of self-employment to come...

CASE STUDY

NAME: **Richard Hewitt** | BUSINESS: **SpinCycle**

Richard Hewitt, 22, has built a bike-powered washing machine for use in the developing world. Finding the time and money to work on a completely new invention is tough, but Richard is about to take SpinCycle Solutions' first prototype to Burundi to test it in the field.

"I went to Burundi in 2010 to visit different charities and network for a church I'm part of. While there I was washing a load of kids' clothes for an orphanage. It's very time-consuming and it can give you a bad back from bending over bowls or in shallow water.

"I realised that bikes were used everywhere and I put two and two together – I thought it would be a good idea to harness the rotary motion of a pedal bike. I was doing a product design degree in Sheffield and I developed the bike-powered washing machine for my graduate project.

"The idea is to sell it to charities in the developing world to supply to communities where there's a need. People can then use it as a micro-business of their own by charging to do laundry."

Richard was was taken on by Gripple, a local manufacturing company who run Incub, a funding and support scheme to help young entrepreneurs develop new products for market. "It was initially for three weeks, but that turned into four months. They haven't taken out equity in my business – it's a bit unusual – but they've given me asupport and access to their workshops."

Richard also received money from Shell LiveWIRE and support from a local laundrette supplier, Goodman Sparks, who got in touch after reading read about him in the local newspaper. They and Gripple are paying for him to go to Africa.

Understanding the market

The difficulty has been getting to the target market to test the SpinCycle. "With most products," says Richard, "you can go to your market with a crude prototype, but it's very expensive to get to Africa. I've tested it as much as I can here, but I still don't really know what's going to happen once I'm in Burundi.

"I've asked charities for feedback and it's clear that it's not going to work everywhere. The challenge for me is finding the communities where it will be a solution to a problem they have."

The business side of it has also been a challenge, says Richard. "I've always wanted to run my own business, but I didn't really understand everything it takes. Gripple took me through what's involved and how to be really strategic about it with six and 12 month plans."

"Currently I'm working full-time, which isn't ideal, but I'm seeing how a bigger business works and starting from the bottom rung of the ladder. I've realised that you've got to do your time learning the ropes and seek help in the areas where you are weakest.

"Next month I've got the test for whether the SpinCycle is actually going to work in the developing world. I think it can make a big difference and has potential to do other things as well. In a year, I'd like to have another application developed that's self-financing. I want to be captain of my own ship, but I've got some more lessons to learn first."

● **www.spincycleproject.wordpress.com**

9. STARTING ON A BUDGET AND STRAIGHTFORWARD FINANCE

The StartUp Loan is for up to £2,500 – you'll be pleased to know a business can be started and grown for far less. It has never been more straightforward to build a business on a shoestring and keep on top of finances with basic spreadsheets or software. You probably already have a computer and a mobile phone, so you might not need to buy much more equipment (depending on your business). Here are some tips for keeping costs low.

Start the business from home

Why take on the cost of an office when the spare room/attic/garden shed will do just as well? Think of the money you'll save: no premises, no commute, no overpriced sandwiches at lunchtime ... !

Embrace social media

Make the most of free or low-cost technology tools to raise your profile and make sales. Chapter 12 offers details of the major social media tools and how they can best be used to your benefit.

Beg, borrow and barter!

When starting out, access all the free and discounted resources you can.

THE BEAUTY OF BARTER: Many start-up businesses barter their goods and services, e.g. "I'll produce a sales brochure for you, in exchange for a handmade cushion for my living room." This works well – both parties get what they want. But take heed of the tax implications. Bartering means money doesn't show up in your accounts, but there has been an exchange of goods and services which implies a taxable activity. The taxman could view bartering as a way to avoid tax. Nevertheless, with so many beneficial arrangements underway, maybe it's time they revised the tax situation?

Access Deals

This StartUp Loans Kit comes complete with tons of deals and offers from leading brands. You can view all of them from page 171 onwards and activate them online at **www.enterprisenation.com/slk**.

Source other deals on the StartUp Britain marketplace (**www.startupbritain.org**), via daily deals site Huddlebuy (**www.huddlebuy.com**), and at Student Beans (**www.studentbeans.com**).

Not only does Student Beans offer relevant deals to students, it was a start-up itself seven years ago ...

CASE STUDY

NAME: **James Eder** | BUSINESS: **The Beans Group**

Seven years after starting Student Beans with his brother Michael, James Eder finds himself director of a company with 30 employees working out of a headquarters in North London. His secret to success is plain old hard work.

"I started Student Beans in 2005 when I was 22, just a few weeks after graduating from the University of Birmingham. I did a business plan as part of my degree, where I actually came up with the idea for the company. After graduating it made sense to set it up."

Having grown up in the age of the internet, Michael knew that when students arrived in a new city, they would turn to the web for help. "Being in an unfamiliar city and living on a limited budget is tough. The internet and a little entrepreneurialism on our part could solve that problem for them."

The company claims to make life "a little more awesome for university students" by providing the latest deals and discounts on eating out, entertainment and travel as well as offering money-saving advice. Since it started, the company has signed up over half a million students and attracts over 800,000 visitors to the site every month.

The company has carried out successful campaigns in the last 12 months, including a recent student Battle of the Bands competition which attracted over 70,000 votes. The Student Sex Survey was the most popular content on Student Beans in 2011, with almost 200,000 page views. It also received media coverage in over 25 publications, including national newspapers.

James's company is now called The Beans Group, and they've recently launched a site called More Beans, focusing on life after university.

At the start

It was with help from The Prince's Trust that the company was first able to get up and running.

"We were looking for an initial start-up loan to get our idea off the ground and had been rejected by the bank. In the end we received a low interest loan from The Prince's Trust. We were part of the Prince's Trust Business Programme and the advice and support from them in the early days was invaluable. It was not just about the funding, but the additional support structure."

Looking ahead, the company has exciting plans including the world's first National Online Freshers' Fair, Freshersfields.com, creating a directory of local student-friendly businesses in university towns and cities and a student money survey. Plus an *Incredibly Simple Guide to Starting Uni*.

You could say this busy and growing team is full of beans!

● www.studentbeans.com | @studentbeans

TOP TIP: "Don't take no for an answer – keep going and have persistence. Also, be prepared to work. So many people come out of university and say, 'I'm going to be an entrepreneur' – but I don't think they realise how many hours you need to put in. And finally, take responsibility. Whether you're working for someone else or yourself, people always find blame and are full of excuses. The only common factor between everything you do is ultimately yourself."

These tips and techniques will help your budgeting, but if you think you'll need more funding in addition to your StartUp Loan, here are a few places to look.

Funding

Friends and family

Friends and family are people you can trust – and asking them for money hopefully won't come with strings attached. Do consider having a written agreement, though, that covers the amount borrowed and a payback schedule.

The bank

Ask to speak to a small business advisor at your local bank . Take a copy of your business plan with you and be prepared to talk it through. Telling them that you have received a StartUp Loan from the government is likely to help your case, as it means you will have already made it through a business plan application process.

A CLEAR DIVISION: Open a bank account early on so you don't mix up your business and personal finances, which may complicate record keeping. Depending on your loan distribution agency, you may be eligible for an account as part of your package.

Crowd funding

Crowd funding is fast becoming a popular route to secure follow-on funding. It involves sourcing funds from a crowd of others. Check out the following links for sites that offer this service.

- CrowdCube | www.crowdcube.com
- Seedrs.com | www.seedrs.com
- ThinCats | www.thincats.com
- IWOCA | www.iwoca.co.uk (for online retailers only and for working capital as opposed to start-up funding)

Shelling out the funds

Apply to the Shell LiveWIRE Grand Ideas Awards to top up your StartUp Loan with an additional £1,000. Four awards are made each month to anyone aged 16 to 30 who is starting a business in the UK or within their first 12 months of trading.

- www.shell-livewire.org/awards

See page 119 for more details on Shell LiveWIRE and other awards to enter.

Investors

Angel investors and venture capitalists can help raise large amounts of start-up funding or development capital for businesses looking to grow. It might be an idea to consider this route further down the line. It doesn't have to be a gruesome experience (à la *Dragons' Den*), though, as there are plenty of funds and investors out there who are eager to part with their money and back good ideas.

Visit the Business Finance For You website (www.businessfinanceforyou.co.uk), which offers details on available grants and funds, searchable by your local area.

In the words of an Angel

Andy Yates is an experienced angel investor and serial entrepreneur. In terms of what he looks for, he says:

"Great businesses are created by great people. I always look out for the three Ps –passion, personality and perseverance. I also back entrepreneurs who really listen and learn. The ability to be flexible, take on board advice and feedback and adapt a product or service to win customers is the real key to unlocking success."

- Angels Den | www.angelsden.co.uk
- Funding Circle | www.fundingcircle.com
- Find Invest Grow | www.findinvestgrow.com
- Springboard | www.springboard.com
- British Business Angels Association | www.bbaa.org.uk

See page 161 for details on accelerator programmes that will take your business from start to growth at speed.

Straightforward finance

When planning a business you'll want to be sure earnings are higher than outgoings. Earnings are also referred to as revenue, turnover or income and this should be a greater figure than outgoings, overheads or costs. Let's look at the items that come within each category.

Incoming

Earn from selling your product or service and any associated income opportunities. For example, you set up a business selling unique handmade cushions. From the outset, earn income from:

- Selling 24 x handmade cushions at £25 per cushion = £600 income per week
- Speaking at events to teach others how to make cushions = £150 per event
- Custom requests, e.g. a unique and one-off production = £75 per item
- Developing a blog on the topic of cushions that attracts cushion-istas as readers and paying advertisers as your customers – £priceless!

Outgoings

Here are the costs; some payable at start-up stage and others ongoing:

- **Salary** – how much do you need to pay yourself? (You will be pleasantly surprised at how thriftily you can live when not commuting.)

- **Property** – start the business from home and avoid the cost of a pricey office.

- **Raw materials and equipment** – what are the materials you need to deliver and promote your finished cushions? And do you need any equipment to make that product; a sewing machine, computer, printer, smartphone or camera?

- **Insurance** – be insured from the start and choose a policy that covers all your needs.

- **Website/promotion materials** – we will cover in Chapters 10–12 how you can build a home on the web and promote the business on a shoestring of a budget.

Keep records of 'Incoming' and 'Outgoing' in a basic Excel spreadsheet as in the following. See pages 152–5 for an example invoice and how to keep a record of invoices raised and amounts paid.

INCOMING	
Product sales	£xx
Sponsorship/Advertising	£xx
Other contracts	£xx
OUTGOINGS	
Salary	(£xx)
IT	(£xx)
Office	(£xx)
Raw materials/equipment	(£xx)
Insurance	(£xx)
Marketing & promotion	(£xx)
Other	(£xx)
PROFIT	**£XX**

II. LAUNCH

You have your idea. It's supported by research and a plan pointing you in the right direction. You've sorted out all the technology you need to get going. And with the company registered, it's time to get into business by making sales and some noise.

> "Be a sponge: absorb as much help and support as you can! Approach others. Listen. Join a networking group. All too often I see entrepreneurs over-protective of their venture. They miss vital guidance."

– Claire Young, founder, School Speakers

10. CREATE A FIRST IMPRESSION

You may have started out by making sales to friends and family who know and trust you to deliver. To attract new customers, it's important to create the right first impression, whether that customer meets you at an event or visits your home on the web. Here's guidance to getting it right and offering a professional welcome.

Your home on the web

You have the tools and connection to get online. The first thing to do is build a presence through a blog, website or store. Not only is a website your window to the world and home on the web, it has become an essential requirement for any new business. Your site can be used as a powerful marketing tool and a way to make money. Having the right technology and knowledge allows you to build, develop and maintain your site. And you can do it all in-house.

Let's look at the three main ways to develop a professional-looking online presence.

1. Blogging

Blogging is a website or part of a website that's regularly updated by an individual or a group of bloggers. There are blogs on any number of topics and the fact that anyone can start blogging for free makes the medium diverse and exciting.

It's an easy way to get online, as you write posts on your topic of choice, upload images and video, and become the go-to place for customers looking for your advice/tips/services/products. Search engines love blogs and the more you write, the higher up the search-engine ranks you will go. Writing regularly is likely to lead to a loyal readership and it's an effective way to communicate your news with existing and potential customers. Readers can add their comments to your entries if you allow them, and you can use your blog to answer questions and establish yourself as an expert in your field.

IT'S FREE AND EASY to get blogging:

- Blogger | www.blogger.com
- TypePad | www.typepad.com
- WordPress | www.wordpress.com

See Chapter 11 for details on how to make money from your blog.

Now you see me

After getting to grips with blogging, why not try your hand at vlogging? This stands for video blogging and is an effective way to interact with customers who want to see you, your products and other happy customers. Vlogging expert, Niamh Guckian, offers tips on how to vlog like a pro:

VLOG HOW-TO

"Vlogging can help you tell people your story: a demonstration of your skills, an atmosphere piece, or an interview.

THE GEAR: "Become an expert on your chosen camera, whether a phone or something fancier.

"Where possible use manual control with your camera – this applies to white balance, exposure and focus. Learn the rules and *then* have fun breaking them.

"Use focus and depth of field to add style to your shooting. Using a tripod sets your work apart from amateur shooting and allows for good steady shot composition.

SAFETY: "Using a small camera can make you feel like you can take risks that you wouldn't otherwise. This has advantages at times but don't take unnecessary risks. Don't shoot from rooftops or get into water!

LIGHT: "As a video-blogger, you will mostly be working with available or natural light. Try to get the most from what's available at the time.

SOUND: "Audio recording is a specialist art form. What we need to achieve as self-shooters is clean and non-distorted sound. Distorted audio is not fixable, and can usually be prevented.

INTERVIEWS: "If your piece is interview-based, engage with the contributor, communicate with them and let them know clearly what you want them to do. Create an atmosphere where the contributor is comfortable, and make sure they know they can stop and start again, or ask questions.

"Make sure the interview is a sequence, that it has a beginning, middle and end, and can stand alone if necessary.

EXPORT AND UPLOAD: "Learn about the optimum settings and platforms for your finished piece."

2. Your own website

Build your own website that you can spec to your own requirements or invest in a template website. Let's look at both options.

DIY

You have decided to build your own site or have a developer take care of it for you.

The first thing to do is buy a domain. A domain makes up a part of your website and email address. So, for example, the domain name I own is enterprisenation.com. My website address is **www.enterprisenation.com** and my email address is **emma@enterprisenation.com**. Both use the enterprisenation.com domain name.

A domain isn't only your address on the web, it's also a big part of your brand, so think carefully when choosing one. There are domain registration companies whose websites allow you to check for available domain names and often suggest available alternatives.

Registering a domain name doesn't give you a website, just an address for it (and an email address). Think of it like reserving a car parking space. You've got the space, now you need to buy the car!

A hosting company will sort you out with the web space to host your site. This is measured in megabytes and gigabytes, just like the information on your computer.

In terms of how much web space you will need, basic hosting packages offer about 250 MB of space, but anything over 1 or 2 GB is more sensible and will also allow you to handle more traffic as your website grows more popular.

With a domain name and web space, potential customers should be able to type your website address into their browser and find out all about your business – just as soon as you've built your site. Finding a hosting company shouldn't be hard.
Most domain registration companies, including those mentioned above, offer web space as a package; and hosting companies usually offer domain registration, too.

1&1 Internet Ltd
www.1and1.co.uk

123-reg
www.123-reg.co.uk

Easily Ltd
www.easily.co.uk

When it comes to hiring a designer, have a think about what you'd like your website to do for your business. The easiest way to start is to think of your website as a brochure, but remember to include the following pages at the very least.

PAGES TO INCLUDE

- **About us**: the story behind your business and its mission.
- **News**: the latest and greatest of your products, business developments, maybe a topical focus if relevant to your business.
- **Products or services**: punchy with the detail, using images of your best work, and text and video testimonials from satisfied customers.
- **FAQs**: questions which you get asked. A lot.
- **Contact us**: email (obviously), but list social media details too.

Choose a designer who has carried out work you like the look of and for companies in a similar kind of sector to your own. That way, the designer will understand what site you're after – and what your kind of visitor will be looking for, as well as how they like to browse and buy.

BRIEF A WEB DESIGNER/DEVELOPER

Here's Emily Hewett's (**www.birdsontheblog.co.uk**) advice on how best to brief a web designer/developer:

"WHO ARE YOU? Give a short summary of who you are and what you do. This will help the designer tune in to your particular sector. Yo'll also need to tell them about your market and how you fit into the larger scheme of things – e.g. competitors, local and national.

"WHAT DO YOU WANT TO ACHIEVE? For example: data capture, sales generation, footfall increase, etc.?

"WHO ARE YOU TALKING TO? Outline a profile of your customer. Who are you targeting? Break it down in terms of sex, age, average income and location.

"WHAT TONE ARE YOU USING? Deciding on how you speak to your audience is important. You may be writing the copy yourself or you may have a copywriter to do this for you. In this section of the brief tell the designer if it's a laid back chatty tone or formal. The tone of the copy needs to be reflected in the design.

"WHAT ARE YOUR LIKES AND DISLIKES? Provide examples wherever possible. It might be a certain colour palette or illustration style or it could be a format. Any of these things help the designer understand what you're looking for.

"ARE THERE ANY MANDATORY ELEMENTS? Fonts, colours, logos, legal text, images, etc. This way they can make sure they produce something on-brand, adhering to your corporate image.

"WHAT'S YOUR BUDGET? A good designer won't take a large budget and fit a job to it. They should find the most cost-effective way of producing exactly what you want. But if you have a small budget, the designer will have to make decisions based on that.

"WHEN DO YOU WANT IT? Make sure the deadline is clear.

"HAVE YOU COVERED EVERYTHING? Show the brief to a colleague or friend to see if they understand it. Once happy, send or talk it through with your designer and invite questions so they are aware you are approachable and that you are both working from the same list of requirements.

Richard Hurtley of Rampant Sporting has made a great success of selling online and in real-world shops ...

CASE STUDY

NAME: **Richard Hurtley** | BUSINESS: **Rampant Sporting**

Richard Hurtley started his clothing brand Rampant Sporting in 2007, aged 22. From humble beginnings selling rugby socks from a garage in Exeter, the company has grown to an online shop, two bricks-and-mortar stores and a distribution network that sees their clothes sold in 80 shops.

"It started off during my third year at university with four pairs of rugby socks. No one else was doing it at the time, selling stylish rugby socks as luxury casual wear. There were just two of us at the beginning and we put in about £2,000 each. We tried getting bank funding and approached six banks, but without success. They all loved it, but it was a case of 'Computer says no'.

"We launched online initially but we were using a garage for storage space so we turned that into a salesroom as well. Then we started supplying an independent clothing store in Exeter on a sale or return basis and we ended up being one of their best-selling brands."

From socks, Richard and friends created a small clothing collection. Growth has been quick, and they now have 45 accounts in the UK. "This puts us in 80 stores – plus we have two shops of our own and we sell through our own and other people's websites." Rampant Sporting now employs 25 people, 15 of them full-time.

Learning how to build a business

When starting out Rampant Sporting got support from the innovation centre at the University of Exeter, where, says Richard, "there's a lot of business knowledge".

"We did plenty of market research and work on the business plan to make sure the idea was sound and we knew where we were going. That thought process is important when you're starting out. And I went to numerous workshops because I had to learn about areas of business that didn't really interest me. I've also recruited around my weaknesses – if you want to become the best you need to have the best people around you.

"My advice to others would be to talk to lots of people. Knock on as many doors as you can. But you need to have a thick skin– entrepreneurship is a difficult journey, especially when you're young and more likely to be written off by others. The joke in our family is that my granny thought the idea was rubbish and I should have a safe job in London. Now she laughs about it – but at the time it gave me real drive to show her that Rampant Sporting was a good idea."

- **www.rampantsporting.com** | **www.facebook.com/rampantsporting** | @rampantsporting

Template site

If DIY feels and sounds too much like hard work, there are a number of companies offering template websites that come with domain registration, hosting, e-commerce and a basic level of design as part of the package. Here are some template site providers offering websites that can be set up today and trading by tomorrow.

IN THE KIT

Launch yourself in the ecommerce world with a special discount and no PayPal fees for 30 days from ekmPowershop and PayPal.

Many e-commerce platform sites come with an in-built payment system. Here are the main ones.

PayPal

Regarded as the leading international payment platform, PayPal has more than 100 million active registered accounts and is available in 190 markets, meaning you can successfully trade in all these markets!

For online store owners, PayPal is easy to introduce and offers customers peace of mind that payment will be secure.

The company offers three main products: website payments standard, website payments pro and express checkout. To enable your customers to buy multiple items, use a free PayPal shopping cart. To put the 'Add to Cart' button on your website you simply copy and paste the HTML code from PayPal to the coding of your own site. Your customers then click the button to make a purchase.

- Add PayPal button | bit.ly/blxrUn

With PayPal, there are no set-up charges, monthly fees or cancellation charges, and fee levels vary depending on the volume of sales.

Google Checkout

Google Checkout is a global payment system. There are no set-up charges and fees depend on the volume of your sales. With monthly sales of less than £1,500, the fee is currently 3.4% plus 20p per transaction. This transaction fee decreases in line with sales volumes increasing.

- checkout.google.co.uk

Sage Pay

Sage Pay is a card payment service that allows you to accept payments by PayPal and major debit and credit cards. It is simple to manage and easy to integrate within your website. The fee is £20 per month for merchants processing up to 1,000 transactions per quarter and 10p per transaction for merchants processing more than 1,000 transactions per quarter, with a minimum charge of £20 per month. There are no set-up fees, no percentage fees and no annual charges.

- www.sagepay.com

Actinic (www.actinic.co.uk)	Actinic Express. £1 set-up fee and £15 per month thereafter for the bronze and basic package.	Company has been established in UK since 1996 and has built a solid reputation. Free 30-day trial on offer.
Big Cartel (www.bigcartel.com)	It's free to present five products, with monthly packages increasing to $29.99 per month for displaying up to 300 products.	With its strapline 'Bringing Art to the Cart', US-based Big Cartel has a focus on providing online stores for clothing designers, record labels, jewellers and crafters.
Create (www.create.net)	Packages start from £2.99 per month. 30-day free trial available.	Set up your site in minutes and benefit from email support plus online forums.
CubeCart (www.cubecart.com)	From free to £110, depending on the features required. Free 30-day trial on offer.	E-commerce shopping cart used by more than one million store owners – so they must be doing something right!
Moonfruit (www.moonfruit.com)	A basic site is free to build, moving up to £22.50 per month for premium options.	The company launched its most recent product Moonfruit Shopbuilder in October 2011, which automatically creates a store on Facebook and a mobile version of your site. The company has created 4.8 million sites.
Mr Site (www.mrsite.com)	Three packages: £24.99 Beginner, £39.99 Standard, £99.99 Professional	You can buy the product in boxed or email format. Helpful tips on how to start via the site.
osCommerce (www.oscommerce.com)	Free	An open source solution with, to date, over 6,800 add-ons available for free to customise your store and increase sales.
SupaDupa (supadupa.me)	Price packages start free and then move through Plankton ($19 per month), Cod ($29 per month) and Caviar ($99 per month).	'Boutique e-commerce for creative minds' comes with the promise these sites will be easy to use and stylishly display your goods. You could spend a while on the main site browsing through what are beautiful looking boutiques.

MAKE YOUR WEBSITE LEGALLY COMPLIANT

These tips are offered by Joanna Tall, founder of
www.OfftoseemyLawyer.com

1. DISPLAY TERMS OF USE

"Think of your website like a board game you are about to play with your visitors. They arrive and are ready to play and you need to state the rules or else it will be chaos! So, for example, state what they can and cannot do – e.g. may they copy your materials? May they link to you? May they rely on the information you provide without double-checking with you or elsewhere? What liability are you prepared to accept? Provide a link to your terms of use, ideally on every page of your website or under a 'Legals' section.

2. DISPLAY YOUR PRIVACY POLICY

"Most websites collect personal data on their visitors either by getting them to register on the site or sign up for a newsletter. By law you must tell visitors what you will be doing with this data and the best way to do this is to set out the information in a privacy policy. Again, a link to it on every page is best. More complex rules apply if you plan to collect sensitive information or information from children, or want to pass the information to third parties; for this you should consult a lawyer. Additionally, you are likely to need to register as a data processor under the Data Protection Act. Simply go to **www.ico.gov.uk** for more information.

3. IF SELLING GOODS OR SERVICES ONLINE, DISPLAY YOUR TERMS OF SALE

"Just as with the board game example, you need rules for selling your goods or services. Most importantly, you need to get your visitors to acknowledge that they accept them. So ideally get them to tick a box stating that they accept them before they proceed to check out. You also need to draw their attention to their rights under the Distance Selling Regulations, e.g. cancellation rights amongst others.

4. PROTECT YOUR COPYRIGHT IN THE WEBSITE CONTENT

"Although you automatically own the copyright in the content that you create, best practice is to remind your visitors! Say, for example: "Copyright 2012 Lawyers R Great Ltd". And if your logo or name is trademarked, broadcast the fact! After all, you will have spent money in getting it that far and it will enhance your brand in the market.

5. STATE WHO YOU ARE!

"By law you need to state a full postal address and contact number and if you are a limited company, the company's registered address, number and country of registration. This also applies to your emails."

Distance Selling Regulations

One thing to bear in mind when selling goods or services to consumers via the internet, mail order or by phone, is compliance with the Consumer Protection (Distance Selling) Regulations 2000. The key features of the regulations are:

- You must offer consumers clear information including details of the goods or services offered, delivery arrangements and payment, the supplier's details and the consumer's cancellation rights before he or she buys (known as prior information). This information should be provided in writing.

- The consumer has a period of seven working days from delivery of the items to cancel their contract with you.

These regulations only apply when selling to consumers, as opposed to businesses. In the event of a contract being ceased, you have to refund money, including delivery charges, within 30 days of the date of cancellation.

- Distance selling regulations | **tinyurl.com/distancesellingregs**

3. A presence on other sites

Maybe you'd prefer to start raising your profile and making sales via other established platform sites, as opposed to your own. Whether selling homemade crafts or business concepts, there are a number of options.

The upside is that these sites attract customers on your behalf, and some of them attract customers from all over the world. Here are six sales platforms that enable you to sell.

eBay

eBay is the largest shopping mall on the web. In 2010 there were 160,000 registered businesses trading on the site in the UK, generating sales of £1.6 billion a year. The good thing is, having a store on eBay means you are opened up to an international audience and many potential customers!

- www.eBay.co.uk

EBAY EXPERTISE

*Dan Wilson (***www.wilsondan.co.uk***) offers five tips on how to make the most of the mega marketplace known as eBay:*

1. START SMALL

"Go slow until you've found your way. Start with a few, easy-to-post items and learn about eBay before boosting your range and prices. Don't stake too much on your first eBay bet.

2. SELL LIKE YOU MEAN IT

"The eBay marketplace is competitive and you'll lose out unless you have top-notch listings. Craft fabulous item titles, make impeccable pictures and write descriptions that tempt buyers. Be truthful and honest and look professional from the start.

3. BE QUICK OFF THE MARK

"Buyers have come to expect great service. Dispatch orders quickly — preferably within 24 hours of payment — and well packed, and make sure you reply to emails and other communications swiftly, too. The quality and speed of your replies and dispatches has an impact on customer feedback.

4. PUT A LID ON POSTAL COSTS

"Understand postage and packaging costs and make sure you factor it in to your costs where necessary.

5. LOYALTY MEANS PROFIT

"When you're building your eBay business, encouraging repeat buyers is important. Once a buyer trusts you as an online seller, they're likely to keep coming back. Offer discounts and incentives with every dispatch and cross-market complementary products."

Alibaba

Having a presence on this site enables you to buy and sell with, and source supplies from, companies across the globe. The site has visitors from 240 countries and regions, with over 1 million registered users in the UK. Through the site you can locate suppliers or make sales of your finished product direct to customers. Alibaba is a champion of international trade; carrying out research on the topic, providing a platform for traders to interact, and promoting overseas sales as a form of business that is wholly viable, regardless of company size.

- www.alibaba.com | @AlibabaTalk_UK

Amazon Marketplace

You may be used to buying from Amazon, but have you considered the site as a platform from which to sell? Have your products appear before millions of customers all around the world by signing up to Amazon Marketplace. It offers two sales options: a package for casual sellers who expect to sell less than 35 items a month (a fixed fee per sale plus a referral fee), and, for more seasoned sellers, there is the 'sell a lot' package, which has a monthly charge plus a referral fee for unlimited sales that do not have to be in the Amazon catalogue.

- www.amazon.co.uk/marketplace

Etsy

With its tag line 'Your place to buy and sell all things handmade' this is still the mother of all craft sites. Since the company launched in June 2005, more than 500,000 sellers from around the world have opened up Etsy shops and buyers of Etsy-listed products span more than 150 countries. During March 2012, the value of goods sold via the site was $62.8 million; a 41.5% increase on March 2011 figures. The desire from consumers to buy all things handmade appears to keep on growing!

To start selling on Etsy you need to register for an account (this requires a credit card and valid email address for verification purposes) and then it costs 20 cents to list an item for four months. When your item sells, you pay a 3.5% transaction fee. For anyone who makes handmade items, the power of this global platform cannot be denied. See pages 85–91 for a listing of handmade marketplaces you can try today, and read the story of Maria Allen on page 92, who started out with an Etsy store as the launchpad for her jewellery business.

- www.etsy.com | @etsy

Facebook

With more than 30 million users in the UK, a significant number of your present and potential customers spend time on Facebook every single day. If your business isn't there, it's missing out. Countless small business owners in the UK use Facebook to quickly and cost-effectively grow their company. The easiest way to start is through having an effective Facebook Page. Learn how to do this step by step in the free guide *Boost your Business with Facebook*, which also shows how to connect with new fans and make the most of Facebook ads.

- *Boost Your Business with Facebook* | www.enterprisenation.com/facebook-book-offer

See page 132 to read the story of how Morphsuits.com have built their business on Facebook.

iTunes

If you are a creator of audiobooks, a publisher of podcasts or developer of apps, then the iTunes platform is your route to market. For apps, Apple gives 70% of revenues to the seller. As of July 2011 over 15 billion apps had been downloaded from its App Store, making it the world's largest mobile application platform. Become a registered Apple developer for the iPhone (developer.apple.com/iphone) submit audio books to iTunes via Audible.com (www.audible.com) and create iBooks for the iPad through the iBookstore. Apple is opening up a world of opportunity for content creators and app developers.

● www.appple.com/itunes

Recent university graduates Jermaine Hagan and Dennis Owusu-Sem have seen first-hand the power of building a business on iTunes …

CASE STUDY

NAME: **Jermaine Hagan and Dennis Owusu-Sem** | BUSINESS: **Revision App**

Jermaine Hagan and Dennis Owusu-Sem are the co-founders of Revision App, which allows students to revise on the go. It's the number-one education app in the UK.

Jermaine and Dennis explain the thinking behind the business:

"A majority of students now have a smartphone and spend time waiting idly in queues, on public transport or before class. This time could be spent on revising (even a quick refresh of a mathematical formula may help with memory), but books and revision packs are too cumbersome for such short snatches. Creating Revision App seemed the perfect solution."

Jermaine and Dennis talked over the idea with friends. They asked what peers wanted to see in a revision application and which subjects should be covered. They then started building it, and soon had it launched for free on the App Store. Next came spreading the word.

"In the early days," they explain, "customer acquisition was focused on the most popular social media platforms. We started by creating a website, YouTube videos and Twitter and Facebook fan pages."

Word of mouth amongst students has also been instrumental. "We aim for organic growth driven by positive reviews from our users. By finding out what they like/dislike about our app we can make iterations on our product. We hope to uncover the most beneficial ways to succeed in exams based on user feedback. We want Revision App to transform the way exams and revision are viewed by all students."

"Ultimately, our long-term goal," Jermaine and Dennis say, "is for Revision App to be the 'go to' application for all students to use to ace their exams."

- **www.revisionapp.co.uk** | @revisionapp

TOP TIP: "Just do it. If you don't try, you've already failed!"

HANDMADE **marketplaces**

A growing number of sites are dedicated to helping the young artisan and handmade business owner sell goods across the globe.

Etsy – **www.etsy.com**

"The world's handmade marketplace" (and a great place to start your selling).

How does it work?

1. You list the item on Etsy for a fee. It costs 20 cents (roughly 12p) to list an item for four months.

2. Shoppers then find your item, and purchase it from you directly, using your payment system which you have set up with Etsy, for example PayPal. Etsy takes a 3.5% transaction fee from the total price of each sale.

3. You then ship the item directly to your customer.

Getting started

Setting up a shop on Etsy is easy and should only take a few minutes: www.etsy.com/join

You will need to enter your Etsy username here, which will be displayed to customers looking at your products. Remember to think about your branding and how you want to present yourself to potential customers when entering these details.

Paying fees

All of your fees will be paid using the credit card you list when you register, or the PayPal account you link to your Etsy account. Etsy will calculate your fees on a monthly basis and email you with a list of payments that are due. You can also pay your bill manually through your account.

Community

Etsy has a thriving community where sellers, artists and creators all come together to share their work and ideas with one another. Etsy also run events such as Craft Nights, which could be a great way to meet other crafters and promote your products to a receptive audience.

The site has a blog which highlights new product launches and new initiatives, plus featured sellers and debates on various topics. Forums feature strongly on the site.

Not On The High Street –
www.notonthehighstreet.com

"One basket, hundreds of unique shops"

How does it work?

Not On The High Street offers you the chance to promote and sell your product under the umbrella of their brand and be supported by their in-house team. They look after all of the e-commerce, administration and marketing elements of selling through the site, so all you need to worry about are the products.

Not On The High Street differs from a number of other platform sites in that they are very selective about who sells with them and decline over 90% of applications.

Membership packages vary but the basic package allows you to add 30 products to your own store, with your own logo, company name and URL.

Getting started

If you're interested in getting set up with NOTHS, you will need to take some photographs of your products and submit these using the online application form.

Applications can take up to seven working days to be processed. After that time you will be contacted by a member of the team.

Folksy – **www.folksy.com**

"Folksy is a place to buy handmade things, and for makers to sell their work and find supplies. Based in the UK, Folksy aims to reclaim craft and showcase talented makers and their work."

You can sell craft supplies on Folksy as well as handmade goods, so long as they are listed as 'supplies' and not in the 'handmade' category.

How does it work?

1. It costs 20p to list an item for 180 days or until the item is sold.

2. Shoppers purchase from you directly, using your payment system which you have set up with Folksy, for example PayPal, or you can accept other payments, such as cash or cheques at your own discretion. Folksy takes a 5% commission fee from the total value of each sale.

3. You then ship the item directly to your customer.

Getting started

The first thing you need to do is decide on the username for your shop. This can't be changed so think carefully about your branding and how you want to appear to prospective customers.

Once your item is listed, customers can start viewing and purchasing. When an order is received you will get an order from Folksy with all the buyer's details and the information about the product ordered. You will also receive notification to say payment has been completed. You then ship the product directly to the customer.

Paying fees

You settle fees through the Your Account section of the website. The total shown will be made up of billed and unbilled fees as well as the 5% commission on sales.

Community

Folksy features a blog which gives updates on important news and events. The site also has a forum where members can discuss craft tips, as well as events, ideas for your shopfront and anything else that takes your fancy!

DaWanda – en.dawanda.com

"DaWanda is the place for unique and individual products and people. Buy handmade and hard to find goods, share your discoveries with your friends and create your own collections."

How does it work?

List your items on the site and set up your own shop which gives you the option of a direct URL – nice and easy to promote to your customers!

People will browse your listings and when someone orders a product you receive an email. You check the details of the order, making a note of any special requests from the buyer, and once happy to go ahead you click to confirm the order, so the buyer can see the final price and pay you. You then ship the item directly to the customer using the method you have specified in the listing.

Getting started

With DaWanda you can set up your own shop for free – all you need to do is provide a name and set up shop categories. You can create your own shop window at this stage to show off the key items in your shop. As soon as this has been established, you can start listing your items and selling to customers!

DaWanda also features something called the DaWanda widget, a tool for displaying your shop on your own website or blog.

Paying fees

DaWanda charges a 5% commission on all sales but does not charge for listing products. Once your fees reach €5, DaWanda will email you an invoice with instructions on how to pay.

Community

The website features the News Bulletin Board as well as a blog, ideal for getting all the latest information on what DaWanda offers and what's popular on the site. The forums are a great place to chat with other crafters and there are also video, social media and Gift Detective areas.

ArtFire – www.artfire.com

"The Premier handmade marketplace to buy and sell handmade crafts, supplies, vintage and art"

How does it work?

Set up your shop and list as many items as you want, with up to 10 photographs per item.

The customer will browse your shop and place an order. You receive the customer's payment and also their delivery details in order to ship the product.

Getting started

You can set up your shop for free at – **www.artfire.com/ext/register/account**.

You then pay nothing for 30 days, and after that the rate is a £7.56 a month for unlimited listings. ArtFire do not take a commission on sales.

Paying fees

Fees will be taken from your nominated payment card on the same day each month (the one on which you originally signed up). For example, if you joined on the 5th December, you would be charged your monthly fee on the 5th of every month.

Community

ArtFire has a range of different community options for you to get involved in and interact with other members. There are forums where you can communicate and share ideas with other crafters, as well as ArtDaily, which is an opportunity to learn new crafts and get sound business advice, plus there's the chance to join a guild and earn a guild badge, as well as listen to the weekly podcast from John Jacobs and Tony Ford, giving tips on how to promote your business and use ArtFire to its full potential.

MISI (Make It, Sell It) – www.misi.co.uk

"The home of buying and selling handmade in the UK"

How does it work?

Create a shop with MISI and list your items for free. When you sell a product you will receive an email notification from MISI which will prompt you to log in to see the full details of the sale. Payment can either be by cheque or PayPal, and once payment is received, you ship the product direct to the customer.

Paying fees

MISI charges 20p per listing, which will be added to your account as soon as you start listing items. MISI also take a 3% commission fee on every sale and this is also added to your account. Fees are then payable on a monthly basis.

Community

The MISI community section is broken down into several areas including: a blog where crafters write about their latest ideas, materials and events; a forum for sharing tips and ideas; and a Meet the Maker section where shop-owners and crafters are encouraged to share their experiences with the community.

ShopHandmade – www.shophandmade.com

"Rewarding Creativity"

How does it work?

You can sell your items in five easy steps! Once you have listed your products, customers can browse them and begin buying right away. When an item sells, you're notified by email, and payment is made to your registered PayPal account. You then ship the item using easy-to-print labels from PayPal.

Getting started

List your item for a small fee of 25 cents, and then upload up to five photos per item. Then you need to decide if you are participating in Sales and Galleries and activate your listing.

When you are listing items, there is also the opportunity to get the listing sponsored, which means a third-party sponsor will pay for listing your item, costing you nothing. There are several sponsors to choose from and their sponsorship simply means that a non-intrusive advertisement will appear on your product page.

Paying fees

ShopHandmade only charge a percentage of an item's final selling price. The payment is taken when an item actually sells.

Community

ShopHandmade features blogs from various sellers so that you can see what other crafters are up to and keep track of developments and new ideas in the crafting world.

A TOP QUALITY IMAGE: Whether you decide to start online with a blog or a full e-commerce site, place high quality images on your site and printed materials so that on first click or at first glance, a customer is inclined to buy. Take professional images yourself or consider subscribing to a stock image library such as www.istockphoto.com. Other image libraries include: www.imagesource.com, www.photos.com and www.gettyimages.com. Search for Creative Commons licensed images you can use commercially from Flickr at www.compfight.com.

CASE STUDY

NAME: **Maria Allen** | **BUSINESS**: **Maria Allen Jewellery**

Jewellery-maker Maria Allen graduated from the University of Brighton with a degree in graphic design in 2011 and went straight into self-employment. But she'd already been selling her own creations for years before she started her full-time venture, Maria Allen Jewellery.

"I started making cards when I was 14 and one of my friends said that I should sell them. So from the age of 14 to 18 I was making cards and selling them to shops on the side while at school and college. At university in Brighton I approached some of the little card and gift shops in the Laines and started selling to them as well.

"I've always liked jewellery," says Maria, "and whenever I've gone on holiday I've found interesting pieces that were unique. I taught myself how to make them into jewellery and started selling to friends and then to friends of friends. Then I opened an Etsy shop and found suppliers of charms and jewellery findings so I could make more of the same designs. Finally I set up my own website through Big Cartel, an online shopping cart for artists and makers."

From there, Maria created a wholesale catalogue and started approaching stockists. "Whenever I visit a new place, I drop into boutiques, leave a business card and ask for the buyer's contact details. I'm now stocked in Paris, San Francisco, New York and the Netherlands. I'm always looking for new boutiques to stock my jewellery.

"When I first started running my business full time, I thought that it would be fantastic to have my jewellery in the Tate Gallery shop, so I got in touch with their buyer and she told me about an Alice in Wonderland exhibition. I created a collection based on the original illustrations and she loved it. So my jewellery was in the Tate in Liverpool and the Tate Britain!"

What it's like to run a business

"I didn't think I could ever be self-employed, but when I tried really hard at university, I realised that making jewellery could potentially support me. Both my parents are self-employed and they gave me advice about things like invoicing – plus I use their accountant. With finances, you need to understand what you're doing and what the HMRC needs from you at the end of the year."

Maria has also received mentoring from her local MP and from Dean Walton of Mask-Arade, who was on *Dragons' Den*. "He employs ten people and it was good to see how a bigger business works because my aspiration is to expand my business further.

"You need patience and perseverance to run your own business. Lots of the time you're going to get knocked down, so you need to understand and learn and get back up again. Also, try to get support as much as you can – there's lots out there, whether friends, family or other professionals. I'm constantly getting opinions and advice."

- www.mariaallenboutique.com |
  www.facebook.com/mariaallenboutique |
  www.mariaallen.blogspot.co.uk | @maria_allen

TOP TIP: "The most important thing is to really love what you do. My brain never switches off from my business. I'm always thinking, 'What opportunities could I be missing?'."

Rise up the search engine ranks

Promote your business and website through search engine optimisation. Commonly referred to as SEO, this is the process by which you can improve rankings for your website in the top search engines such as Google, so that your site appears on the first few pages of results rather than on page 75.

Google is a search engine that uses software known as 'spiders' to crawl the web on a regular basis and find sites to add to their index. There are steps you can take to make it easier for the spiders to find and add your site.

THINK LIKE A BUYER: When thinking of the keywords to use in PPC (pay per click) ad campaigns (and in search engine optimisation) think of the words your buyers will be using when searching for your product or service. Use the Google AdWords Keyword Tool to find out the most popular search terms. Apply these words in the campaign and include them in the text on your site.

Start with the homepage

Provide high-quality, text-based content on your pages – especially your homepage. If your homepage has useful information and good quality, relevant text, it's more likely to be picked up by the spiders. Beyond the homepage, write pages that clearly describe your topic/service/product. Think about the words users would type to find your pages and include them on the site.

Make contributions

Identify influential bloggers and sites in your trade/industry, contact them and offer to write posts. You can also improve your visibility by writing helpful comments in forums and on other people's posts.

Be well connected

Improve the rank of your site by increasing the number of other high-quality sites that link to your pages; these are referred to as inbound links. For example, if you're running a competition, go to sites that promote competitions and add yours.

Register your site with the major search engines.

- Google | www.google.co.uk/addurl
- Yahoo! | search.yahoo.com/info/submit
- Bing | www.bing.com/webmaster/submitsitepage.aspx

SEARCH ENGINES LOVE LINKS: Another way to increase your ranking in the search results is to link to other sites and vice versa, but think quality here as opposed to quantity. Sites offering the best 'link juice' are trusted domains, such as news sites, and very popular sites. You could post comments on such sites and blogs and include a link back to your site. Try these handy hints: approach sites complementary to your own and suggest reciprocal links; ensure that your website link is included in all your social media profiles; register with the major search engines (see above); add your domain to local search services such as Google Maps, Qype, Yahoo! Local and BView.

- www.google.co.uk/maps

- www.qype.co.uk

- www.uk.local.yahoo.com

- www.bview.co.uk

Tagging

A webpage's title, referred to as a 'title tag', is part of the SEO mix and can make a difference to your search rankings. It is also the text that appears in the top of the browser window. Include in your title tag the main key phrase you'd like the search engines to associate with your webpage and keep it to 60-90 characters in length. Duncan Green of Moo Marketing is an SEO expert and explains: "the title tag on the homepage for Moo Marketing reads: 'Moo Marketing – Search Engine Marketing – PPC Management – Search Engine Optimisation'. As you can see the title element is 85 characters long, contains three key phrases and identifies the subject of the webpage."

Pay per click advertising

The results from your efforts in SEO will appear on the main engines as a natural or 'organic' search result. But have you spotted results on the right of the page when searching for items yourself? These are paid-for results and referred to as pay per click or PPC advertising. PPC is where you pay to have ads displayed when people type in certain words, in the hope it will attract more visitors to your site.

Google AdWords is a form of PPC advertising. Think of the key words or phrases you reckon your customers will be searching for and apply them in your Google campaign. Link to your home page or other pages on the site where you're running a promotion and make the most of geotargeting, which lets you target your ads to specific territories and languages.

You are in full control of the budget and campaign duration.

- adwords.google.co.uk

Spread the word

Make it easy for visitors to spread word of your site through social sharing. Have your site Stumbled, Dugg and Tweeted and make the most of this viral effect. You can add these social bookmarking tools by visiting AddThis (www.addthis.com) and choosing the icons you'd like to have displayed on your site.

The most popular are:

- Delicious | www.delicious.com

- Digg | www.digg.com

- StumbleUpon | www.stumbleupon.com

Your business in print

Print is far from dead, so get yourself some business cards, postcards and promotion flyers to hand out at business events, social occasions, and to just about anyone you meet! Have fun with designing your cards at www.moo.com and get a range of designs printed in each batch. Sell vintage fashion? Upload pictures of your products to the reverse of each card. Offer web design services? Have a portfolio of sites you've designed there.

IN THE KIT

Get 50 Classic or Green Business cards from **moo.com** for free.

Vistaprint (**www.vistaprint.co.uk**) are also giving away 250 business cards to all kit readers.

Look at my logo!

When you contact potential customers you'll want them to read about you and get a sense of your style. You can do this very effectively with a nice-looking logo or company design that's repeated across all your promotion materials, from business cards to brochures.

Think about what you'd like as your company font, colours and layout. Have a go at designing this yourself or hire the services of a designer/neighbour/friend. Good presentation can make a world of difference. This may just be the difference you need to clinch a contract.

Find a professional to design your logo via these sites:

- CrowdSPRING | www.crowdspring.com
- 99designs | www.99designs.com
- BuildaBrand | www.buildabrand.com
- Concept Cupboard | www.conceptcupboard.com
- Elance | www.elance.com

Office address

If you are running the business from home there are a couple of reasons why you might not want to put the home address on your business card: it might sound too domestic, and you might not want people turning up on your doorstep!

You can solve this with a P.O. Box number, which starts at £185 per year and is easily set up with Royal Mail (www.royalmail.com/pobox). Alternatively, you could invest in a virtual office, which gives you a more tailored and personal service than a P.O. Box – plus you get a nice-sounding address and a place to use for meetings. Having a virtual office enables you to choose the address that suits you best, have post delivered to that location, and then forwarded on to you. Companies providing this service include:

- Regus | www.regus.com
- Bizspace | www.bizspace.co.uk

When holding meetings, consider hiring professional meeting space. Many offer serviced addresses and secretarial services too, so there could be great continuity for your clients if they only have to remember one address.

IN THE KIT

Get one month's free virtual office or one month free in any Bizspace unit.

Get a value business start-up package from Regus.

On the phone

When running the business from home, consider who will be picking up the phone! It's cheap and sometimes free to get an 0845 local rate number or an 0870 national rate number for your business. This will hide where you're based and divert your calls to wherever you specify. But beware: sometimes having such a number – especially with national rates – might put customers off ringing you.

If you use a landline number it's best to have a separate line for your home and your business. These days you don't need to invest in an actual second line. You can use a VoIP (voice over internet protocol) phone, which uses a broadband internet connection to make and receive calls, something we looked at earlier.

- Skype | www.skype.com

Another idea is to get some help from a call-handling service. They will answer your calls with your company name, text urgent messages to you and email the others, giving you a big business feel for about £50 per month. Services on offer include:

- Moneypenny | www.moneypenny.co.uk
- Regus | www.regus.co.uk
- MyRuby | www.myruby.co.uk
- Answer | www.answer.co.uk

You might consider a 'follow-me number' to ensure you're available when you need to be and able to deliver the right impression to clients. A follow-me number involves choosing a number and directing calls from it to your landline or mobile. The beauty of choosing a number is that you have the option to select either a freephone or a geographical number so, say you'd like to have a Manchester area code, simply buy a number starting with 0161. The same goes for hundreds of other locations.

Offer virtual phone numbers where the caller pays a local rate, regardless of where you are, through Vonage (www.vonage.co.uk) or direct calls to you from a chosen number using internet technology and a virtual receptionist at eReceptionist (www.ereceptionist.co.uk).

In person

You are about to attend your first networking event or trade show and want to create a good first impression. With an attractive business card in hand, directing prospective customers to a good-looking online presence, all you have to do is follow the rules of effective networking!

The art of networking

- Wear your name tag (if you have one) on your right side. It's easy to catch sight of when you are shaking hands.

- Deliver a nice firm handshake and make eye contact.

- Say your name clearly and, in under ten seconds, tell the other person who you are and what you do.

- Listen carefully. Ask the other person plenty of questions about their line of business, their hobbies, etc.

- Be positive and energetic.

- Swap business cards.

- Send a thank-you email after the event, confirming any actions you and they have promised.

- Keep in regular and meaningful contact.

See Chapter 12 for details of networking groups to join and for information on how to host your own event or attend a trade show to promote your business.

A MEMORABLE EXCHANGE: Richard Moross, founder of moo.com, says: "The point of having a business card is to make a connection, create a relationship and leave something with the recipient that reminds them of you. Have cards that tell a story. Use that card as a sales tool, for sure, but also show appreciation by having cards relating to your customer." Richard achieves this by having images on his cards showing places he's visited and meals he's eaten. With 70% of moo.com's business being outside the UK, Richard travels a lot and the cards act as the ice-breaker in meetings as he tells the story behind the pictures.

11. MAKE SALES

With a professional image established, you are ready to start making sales. This chapter will help you achieve that first sale, plus provide tips on how to make money from your website or blog.

1. Make a list (check it twice)

Draw on your existing resources, grab your address book and select the friends, family, colleagues and acquaintances you think might be interested in your product or service. Add to the list with details of local people and businesses, too.

2. Pitch up

Contact the people on your list and announce your new business venture. Consider this an opportunity to make your pitch, but don't be too pushy. Remember to address each recipient personally. No one likes a group email!

3. Follow up

Follow up in a few days time, either with another email or, better still, a phone call. Take some soundings as to the success of your pitch and react accordingly. If the potential customer or client sounds keen, go for it! Arrange to meet him or her to show your product or explain more about your service.

4. Meet up

Arrange a time and place to meet that's convenient for your potential customer or client. Be professional, but also likeable. These are equally important characteristics when making a sale.

If the customer agrees the deal, bring the meeting to a fairly speedy end. Your job is done – for now. It's time to head home and deliver on the promise you made with your first customer.

5. Make some noise

Once you've made your first sale – shout about it! If your new customer or client agrees, include them in a press release or write about them on your website or blog, so other potential customers or clients can see that you're well and truly in business!

SALES ARE FLYING HIGH: Have promotional flyers made to take to events or deliver through doors. Increase chances of turning flyers into firm sales by:

- having a design that is memorable, possibly quirky and, ideally, that your potential customers will want to keep on their desk/in their bag/atop the kitchen shelf

- making the offer clear and confirming the benefits of buying

- including a call to action, i.e. a way in which the interested customer can contact you.

Warm up for a cold call

Sales and marketing pro Jackie Wade (www.winningsales.co.uk) offers tips on how to make winning calls to customers ...

"**Ready:** Preparation and focus is key. Start with a call list and clear objectives; which business or household and who specifically are you calling (decision maker)? Are you clear on your message? What benefits do you offer?

"**Steady:** Feel confident, think positive. What's the worst thing that can happen? They may say no... so what! Not everyone out there will want you, but someone will! Tone is more important than words so feel and sound confident and positive.

"**Go:** Be natural, be you. Have a good opening 'hook' to grab attention – something interesting, new or different and make it relevant to the person you're calling. Avoid rambling – focus on a two-way conversation, not a fixed script. Develop a list of open questions which will allow you to engage with the person at the other end of the line, e.g. what do you currently do, how does it work, what might you like to improve? Listen for opportunities. Engage!

"**Grow:** Agree action and follow up promptly or agree a call back, if no interest for now. A NO today may be a YES tomorrow; tenacity counts. Things change.

"Remember, smile and then dial. Your aim is to spread the word about you and your business."

WHEN MAKING A SALES CALL, do so standing up and smiling. To the person on the other end, you will come across as positive and confident.

Selling into physical stores

Maybe you've started by selling products direct to customers at shows and fairs, but what about making sales via local shops?

Before you approach any shops, make a list of appropriate places where you think your product could work well. For example, does your town have gift shops or an art gallery, are there lots of boutiques that stock a range of different items? Think outside the box. Could your local coffee shop stock some of your items?

Five top tips for market placement

Laura Rigney, founder of Pitcher House, is author of *Pitching Products for Small Business* and offers five top tips for pitching your product effectively:

1. Be confident with pricing

"Selling in wholesale is a whole new ballpark as far as pricing is concerned. Make your product attractive to buyers with your pricing. A great way to show you're trying to help retailers is to setup a structured pricing system, i.e. 100 units or less £xx per unit, 101-500 units £xx per unit and 501 units or more £xx per unit. This system could also encourage shops and buyers to place larger orders.

2. Understand your product inside out

"This means technical data as well as knowing why someone would buy it. When you get a meeting with a buyer or approach a shop owner, talk with confidence about where the product is made, by who, and using what kind of materials. Remember there is pressure on large retailers to "go green", so the more you can offer that as a potential supplier the more attractive you will be.

3. Be prepared

"If a buyer places an order, how quickly will you have manufacturing, distribution and storage in place? Buyers won't expect a new small business to have a giant factory sitting waiting for someone to press the 'go' button but they will want a realistic estimate of how long it will be until your product is in their warehouses/on the shop shelf. Once you have given your timings, stick to them. Even if this means exaggerating the time it will take for them to be delivered. Better to be early rather than late!

4. Pitch perfect

"If you're pitching in person, make it informative, exciting and interesting and where possible have evidence of past sales and customer satisfaction. You need to know your figures without having to look through paperwork and be prepared to haggle a little on prices. If someone likes your product enough and you have sold it well enough they will buy it, even if it's a few pennies more than they would like to pay. In the other direction, sometimes it may be worth offering a larger than normal discount as a trial for a first order.

5. Stay listed

"When a company takes on your product it's called being listed. Once you are listed the work is just beginning! It is now time to stay listed for as long as possible and the way to do this is through marketing and PR. The more you promote your product and the shops/galleries/boutiques that are selling them, the more they will be bought by consumers thus encouraging buyers to place more orders with you!"

WATCH OUT FOR HIGH STREET STARTUP, being launched by StartUp Britain to help small businesses get onto the High Street through pitching to large retailers and filling empty stores. Register for the StartUp Britain newsletter (www.startupbritain.org) to be the first to know.

Going Global

Of the 20 young businesses profiled in this kit, 75% are trading overseas; making sales via the platform sites covered on page 81 onwards or selling directly into new markets through local contacts and/or assistance from UK Trade & Investment.

To discover more about the specifics of international trade and how to go global in five basic steps, download a free eBook (tinyurl.com/goglobalguide) which offers all you need to know on topics from customs documentation to website translation and perfecting the art of cultural etiquette. Also take advantage of the DHL offer in the kit to ship goods cost effectively.

IN THE KIT

Get 10% off DHL Servicepoint at Staples Stores.

- *Go Global* eBook |
  tinyurl.com/goglobalguide

- Go Global on Enterprise Nation |
  tinyurl.com/goglobalEN

- DHL blog |
  www.dhlguide.co.uk/news

- UK Trade & Investment |
  www.ukti.gov.uk

Make money from your website

As traffic to your blog increases, so does your chance of generating income. Make a profit from your posts with this top-ten list of options.

1. Display advertising

Offer advertising on your site. The more niche your audience, the more likely you are to attract advertisers.

The information you'll need to provide includes:

- number of unique visitors
- number of impressions
- average duration of visit
- visitor demographics.

Write a basic rate card (see page 109), add it to your site and send it to corporate marketing departments and media-buying agencies.

2. Google AdSense

This tool from Google does the work for you by placing relevant ads on your site and earning you money when people click on them. You can customise the appearance of the ads so they sit well with the style of your site.

- www.google.co.uk/adsense

3. Text Link Ads

These ads offer direct click-throughs from text on your site. You submit your site to Text Link Ads and then upload the ad code provided. It's your choice whether you approve or deny the supplied ads. Once that's done, you start making money as visitors click on the ads. Try this and Skimlinks, which converts words on your site to affiliate links so that you earn from those, too.

- www.text-link-ads.com
- www.skimlinks.com

4. Sponsored conversations

Get paid for posts (and now tweets) with services like IZEA that match bloggers with advertisers. Some doubt the ethical stance of paying a blogger to write something about a product but there's no doubt that it's a money maker.

- www.izea.com

5. Affiliate schemes

Sign up to affiliate schemes like the Amazon Associates Programme, where you can earn up to 10% in referrals by advertising Amazon products. The programme works by driving traffic to Amazon.co.uk through specially formatted links. You earn referral fees on sales generated through those links. Monthly cheques are sent to you from Amazon and it's easy and free to join.

- affiliate-program.amazon.co.uk

6. Sponsored features

This could include a host of options. Approach advertisers with suggestions of a sponsored eBook, e-news, podcast, webchat, poll or survey. These applications can be added to your site at a low cost yet generate good revenue.

For:

- eBook creation, try www.blurb.com
- a survey or poll feature, try www.surveymonkey.com
- email marketing, try www.mailchimp.com

7. Expert help

Offer your expertise and charge people to log on and watch or listen. This could be made available through Teleclasses where you invite customers and contacts onto a call where you offer your expertise on a one-to-many basis. Or deliver a presentation to potentially thousands of paying customers via www.gotowebinar.co.uk.

8. Deals with suppliers

Do deals with suppliers. Hosting a travel blog? Agree a percentage each time a booking is made via your site. Hosting a wedding blog? Create a directory of wedding suppliers such as venues, photographers, dressmakers and caterers with an enhanced listing for those who pay.

9. Turn a blog into a book

Follow the lead of Alex Johnson who turned his Shedworking blog (www.shedworking.co.uk) into a book – and then a second book – which are now selling across the UK and overseas, acting as an effective marketing tool for the site!

10. Please donate

If you'd rather just ask for a small donation from your visitors, this is possible too via a donate feature from PayPal. Add a PayPal donate button to your site: bit.ly/ikf832

* * *

Maybe you've decided to start selling products through your site. But if you only carry content, you'll need to add an e-commerce feature to make sales.

JUST-IN-TIME PAYMENT: Add a PayPal payment button to your site and you'll be able to accept payment from all major credit and debit cards, as well as bank accounts around the world. You can set it up in less than 15 minutes.

Add an e-commerce plug-in

Want to open your site up to sales? Do so by plugging in an e-commerce tool such as:

- WordPress e-Commerce shopping cart – "suitable for selling your products, services, or fees online": bit.ly/fEgQHo

- PayPal Shortcodes – insert PayPal buttons in your posts or pages using a Shortcode: bit.ly/KGNE5f

- View a complete list of WordPress e-commerce plugins: bit.ly/eTEkwZ

Add a shopping cart to your site

Make it easy for your visitors to click and buy. Check out these shopping cart providers:

- GroovyCart | www.groovycart.co.uk
- RomanCart | www.romancart.com
- CubeCart | www.cubecart.com
- Zen Cart | www.zen-cart.com
- ekmPowershop | www.ekmpowershop.com
- osCommerce | www.oscommerce.com
- Frooition | www.frooition.com [shopping cart and full website]

Research the product that suits you best, taking into account hosting provision, back-end admin, and built-in search engine optimisation. For more information on e-commerce, view the video series '10 steps to e-commerce success' produced by Enterprise Nation in association with PayPal: bit.ly/gEdpWO

SHOW ME YOUR RATES! The purpose of a media rate card is to show potential advertisers what your site can deliver to them in terms of traffic and sales. To do this, include some key points:

- **A brief description of the site:** What it does and for whom.
- **Visitor demographics:** Do you have data on the age of your visitors, their home region, gender, etc? If so, include it, as it helps build a picture of your audience.
- **Site traffic:** What are your unique visitor numbers and length of time spent on the site? Make a note if the figures are increasing.
- **Costings:** Do you have a cost-per-click (CPC) or cost-per-impression (CPM) rate? If so, include it here, along with the price of other sponsorship options. Offer a menu but leave some flexibility, with 'costed on a project basis' for sponsor features that would benefit from a more tailored proposal.
- **Screen shots:** Showing how and where adverts or sponsored features appear on the site.

- **Media activity:** Note where you've recently been covered in the media, online and off, so that potential sponsors can see how and where you're promoting the site.

- **Testimonials:** Positive comments from existing sponsors gives you credibility and gives confidence to the next potential sponsor.

- **Team details:** Who are the faces behind the site and what are their credentials? In other words, your background career and activities, etc.

Round this off with your contact details so that interested potential sponsors can get in touch and place an order!

12. MAKE SOME NOISE!

ales are coming in, customers are happy and you want to tell the world about you and your new business. Profile brings new customers and new sales. Get yourself known in the press and online by making friends with the media, hosting events, entering awards and embracing social media.

Here's what to do.

Plot the script

Imagine yourself as the star of your own Hollywood movie. Are you an action hero, battling against the odds (think James Dyson) or a brand leading lady (think Nigella Lawson)? Plot the action and write the script. It will help you define your message to the media.

Find the right contacts

Research the journalists you think are interested in your field. Note their email addresses from the bottom of their articles, follow them on Twitter, get to know them and send them exclusive stories about you and your business.

LINK REQUEST: If you're being featured online ask the journalist if they can include a live link to your site. That way, readers can be on your site with one click.

Write a release

Writing a press release costs nothing but your time, yet it can generate thousands of pounds' worth of publicity. If you're emailing a press release to journalists, write the text in the body of the email and include it in an attachment, too.

Your press release should have an attention-grabbing headline, the main facts in the first sentence, and evidence and quotes from as high-profile people and companies as possible in the main body of the text. Include great quality images wherever you can to lift the piece and put a face to the brand.

You could also use a press-release distribution service to secure wider exposure. My personal favourite is Response Source (www.responsesource.com) but there's also PR Newswire (www.prnewswire.co.uk) and PRWeb (www.prweb.com).

If you don't get a response, follow up!

Beckie Andrews (page 114) chose to employ the services of a PR company so she could raise her profile and have her brand seen in all the right places.

AN IMAGE SPEAKS LOUDER THAN WORDS: When a picture speaks a thousand words you can afford to talk less! Consider hiring a professional photographer to take pictures of you and your work. Maybe you can do this as a barter deal? Or pick up your own digital camera and do it yourself. A journalist is much more likely to cover your story if you have great imagery to go with it. Use the images on your website and in promotion materials, and let your business speak for itself.

Example press release

1. Attention-grabbing headline

2. The first line is punchy and explains the what, who, why and where of the headline

3. Back up the headline and first sentence with more detail – facts and figures if you have them

4. Include a quote from you (or your business partner, if relevant)

5. Can you include a quote from someone else? A happy customer, industry expert or celebrity?

6. End with a call to action. Where can people go to find out more/how to download the report/which site to visit to claim a free gift, etc.?

7. Include 'Notes to Editors', with brief details on you and your company

8. Remember to include contact details – your email address and telephone number

9. Attach a relevant and interesting image

NEW PARTNERSHIP BRINGS $100,000 TO UK STARTUPS

Elance, the internet platform used by businesses to gain instant access to over one million independent workers online, and Enterprise Nation, the small business support company, have partnered, offering UK startups and small businesses over $100,000 to help them grow their companies.

Small businesses will be eligible to receive Elance service credits by attending Enterprise Nation events, accessing the Elance platform from the Enterprise Nation website or participating in online competitions.

"The partnership with Enterprise Nation is an essential component of our expansion into Europe," said Kjetil J. Olsen, Vice President, Europe at Elance. "We are looking forward to participating in events, showcasing companies who are making the most of Elance and enabling business owners to grow a successful company using our global talent marketplace."

Richard Baldock, Managing Director at Desktag, has hired developers on Elance to work on new products for his business. "On Elance, I quickly found experts with the skills I need. I hired developers around the globe, so that means the work is done by the time I start for the day!"

"For some time we have recognised that companies are growing by outsourcing and subcontracting as opposed to hiring staff and Elance offers a route to all the talent you need," said Emma Jones, Founder of Enterprise Nation. "I'm delighted we can make this available via Enterprise Nation in addition to offering thousands of pounds worth of value in credits. It's a great time to be growing a business and this partnership will ensure you do so in the most modern way, whilst staying nimble and keeping overheads low."

To access Elance credits, businesses can head to: **tinyurl.com/ENElance**

Media notes

Elance (**www.elance.com**), the world's leading platform for online employment, helps businesses hire and manage in the cloud.

Enterprise Nation (**www.enterprisenation.com**) is a small business support company and through a website and books, events and a fund, the company helps individuals start and grow small businesses.

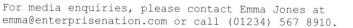

For media enquiries, please contact Emma Jones at emma@enterprisenation.com or call (01234) 567 8910.

Tweet, Tweet

Follow media channels, journalists and personalities on Twitter so you're the first to pick up the news and media requests:

- @BBCBreakfast
- @BBCOnthemoney
- @talktothepress
- @findaTVexpert
- @TheTimes
- @guardian
- #journorequest
- @TheoPaphitis, who runs Small Business Sunday #sbs every week between 5pm and 7.30pm where six lucky companies are re-tweeted. Full details at **tinyurl.com/smallbusinesssunday.**

See page 165 for a top 50 listing of people to follow on Twitter who are involved with all things youth enterprise.

And finally ... please contact Enterprise Nation with your story. We are always profiling start-ups and small businesses on our website, in books (like this one!), in kits, in videos and as part of the national StartUp Britain campaign. Submit your story at **www.enterprisenation.com.**

CASE STUDY

NAME: **Beckie Andrews** | BUSINESS: **Not for Ponies**

Beckie Andrews, 24, launched fashion label Not for Ponies after a year in the childrenswear industry. From trading at craft fairs, to opening a small shop in a Manchester fashion emporium, she now sells her own quirky creations online and through boutiques across the UK. Beckie is also concentrating on building her brand.

"I've wanted to be a fashion designer since I was at primary school. I was always sketching in my spare time and went on to complete a Fashion Enterprise degree. It was fashion combined with business studies. We had to make unique products and sell them at markets.

"Several people around me were self-employed and running their own businesses when I was growing up. I saw how people could be their own boss and make their own decisions. I also saw the other side, too – you have to work long hours. I got a balanced view and naturally progressed into starting my own business.

"I was still working full-time and making things from home, selling products at craft fairs and markets. Then I moved to Manchester, got a studio and started working full-time on the business. After six months, I got a small shop in Afflecks Palace [an emporium of independent traders] and combined my workspace with retail space to cut my overheads.

"I began upcycling vintage clothes as well as making my own, but that's quite time-consuming and costly and doesn't work well online. I was starting to make more sales through the website and stockists, so I closed the shop and went online, focusing on my own designs. I want to do something a bit different and a bit fresher – I want to create my own style."

Building a customer base and brand awareness

"Friends and family were very supportive and I also got advice from a women's business organisation called Train 2000. The mentor they gave me, from a creative background, gave very inspiring but practical advice. I also got start-up funding from Shell LiveWIRE.

"The business side of it – paperwork, accounts, web design – was challenging at first, but you get used to it. The hardest part was building a customer base. My goal is to increase the number of stockists selling my clothes and to increase traffic to my website.

"It's difficult being a new brand and getting into shops. At first I was sending out promotional brochures, but that was time-consuming and costly, so I've eased back on that now.

"Instead, I've got a PR company to raise awareness of my brand and gain press coverage. We're only in the third month of the campaign but it's a lot more promising. I've been in several national magazines and shops are starting to contact me now. I've got several new stockists and a lot more traffic to the site.

"I'm also starting to think about getting international stockists as I get online sales from Europe, America and Australia. Do I prefer working for myself? Most definitely! I like making my own choices and being my own boss."

• www.notforponies.co.uk | www.facebook.com/notforponies | @notforponies

KICK-STARTING WITH PR

Greg Simpson, founder and director of Press for Attention PR (**www.pressforattention.com**) gives his top 12 tips for building a successful PR campaign:

1. HAVE A 'CUNNING PLAN'

"Too many people rush into PR and marketing campaigns with no real plan. You need to consider:

- "What are the goals of the campaign?
- "How do you want to come across in terms of tone?
- "Key messages – what do you want to get across?

2. CONSIDER HOW OTHER COMPANIES GET THEIR MESSAGES ACROSS

"What tactics can you use? PR stunts, press releases, controversy, photo opportunities, comment/opinion pieces, debates, flash mobs, press trips, celebrity endorsements, competitions. There are so many ways to get noticed. Blend them to your requirements and skills.

3. RESEARCH YOUR CUSTOMER/AUDIENCE

"There is little point getting a full article page in *Dog Grooming Monthly* if you sell organic ice cream to boutique hotels! Find out who your ideal customer is and research what they read, listen to and watch. Then, really take the time to read these publications and get to know what sort of stories they publish.

4. FIND THE NEWS HOOK

"Be honest, is your story really news? Examples include: new products, new staff, new promotions, new premises, anniversaries, company expansion, financial milestones and charity efforts.

"You can also provide topical comment on a newsworthy subject. Keep an eye out for issues that affect your business or your customers. This takes practice and you need to establish credibility in your subject area first. Consider starting a blog that provides regular, lively and informed comment in your area of expertise to build your profile. I use WordPress (**www.wordpress.org**), which is free.

5. GOT A STORY?

"Got a story? Great! Now you need a simple press release for a journalist to refer to. People worry that their efforts don't sound flashy enough to warrant attention. But you aren't aiming for a Booker Prize. You're aiming for coherent and interesting *news*.

"Use 'who, what, when, how and why?' as a framework and imagine yourself as the journalist. Is this definitely of interest to their readers? Is it simple enough to understand? Does it stand up on its own?

"I would stick to a maximum of 300 words and keep the press release focused on the news angle.

6. HIT THEM BETWEEN THE EYES

"Journalists get hundreds of press releases every day. Ensure that the headline and first paragraph sum up the entire story in a nutshell. Ideally, your press release should still make sense even if an editor dropped two or three paragraphs.

"I call the journalist beforehand to outline my story. This helps iron out any creases and demonstrates that you are trying to work with them and their audience.

7. DON'T BE TEMPTED TO START HASSLING

"I very rarely 'chase' a journalist once I have sent a press release. If it is good enough, they will use it. Hassling will not push it to the top of the pile and may see it heading towards the recycle bin. Be patient and able to help if the journalist does come back and don't go on holiday the day after you have sent a story out!

8. THINK IN PICTURES

"Consider what makes you read a story when you flick through a newspaper. Headlines play their part but the impact of an interesting picture is greater still. People 'sell' stories, so ensure that anyone in your shot is clearly visible and captioned. Try to show the impact of the news – product shots are okay, but a product in the hands of a customer is better."

9. BUILD A RELATIONSHIP

"PR is not a 'them v us' war with journalists. It's a working relationship, where both parties stand to gain. They get news/insight and you get free publicity in exchange for a fresh take on things or for your role in illustrating the impact of an issue.

10. MEASURE AND EVALUATE

"How do you know if your gym regime and new diet is working? You get on the scales (peeking between your fingers). Are you getting through to the right journalists? How many stories are you sending out? How many are getting coverage? How much coverage do they get? Do your pictures and even your key messages get included? Are you being invited to comment on topical issues?

11. PUT YOUR PR HAT ON AND EXECUTE THE PLAN

"I know many small businesses that freeze when it comes to actually putting their plans into action. Schedule and commit some time every week to do something that contributes to your PR campaign.

12. A FINAL TIP

"PR agencies spend vast amounts on media monitoring software for mentions of their clients or to keep in touch with specific debates. You can do a lot of it for free. Have a play with Google Alerts (**www.google.com/alerts**)."

Enter awards

Enter awards and competitions and enjoy the press coverage that goes with it. Many award schemes are free to enter and are targeted at young start-up businesses. Writing the entry will help to clarify your goals and vision, and winning will bring profile and prizes.

To find out about upcoming awards across the UK, visit: www.startupbritain.org.

Here are some awards that accept entries from 18 to 25 year old business owners:

- Shell LiveWIRE Grand Ideas Awards (www.shell-livewire.org/awards) – up to four awards per month of £1,000 for anyone aged 16 to 30 and looking to get an idea off the ground.

- Ambition AXA Awards (www.ambitionaxaawards.com) – a prize of £40,000 for someone between the age of 11 and 18 who wants to launch a business – that's quite a start-up sum!

- The Pitch (www.thepitchuk.com) – enter regional heats and pitch to experienced judges for a place in the national finals and a £50,000 prize. Takes place across the UK.

- *Country Living* Magazine Kitchen Table Talent Awards (www.kitchen tabletalent.com) – if you're working on a talent or skill from the kitchen table and know it can be turned into a business, this competition is for you. Prizes include office equipment and profile in the magazine, which can be very good for sales!

- Social Enterprise Awards (www.socialenterprise.org.uk/events) – celebrates social enterprises of all ages.

- Nectar Small Business Awards (nectar.com/business-sba2012) – offers cash prizes and plenty of Nectar points!

- Startups Awards (www.startups.co.uk/startups-awards) – celebrating small businesses of all shapes and sizes.

Rise to the challenge

Enter an enterprise challenge developed by the Prelude Group (backed by The Supper Club and Red Bull) and make an impression in the world of business. Rise To was first launched as the Social Enterprise Challenge towards the end of 2009. Now in its fourth year, it is attracting entries from teams across the country, who each have to run a campaign championing a cause that's close to their hearts (previous winners have championed teachers, midwives and paramedics).

The training is delivered in weekly modules online (supported by business mentors) and the team as well as individuals are scored on performance. The key measure of success is how many thanks messages and unique visitors a team can attract to its campaign page within the six-week period.

The best teams and individuals are eligible for prizes and unique work experience shadowing successful entrepreneurs.

Partnering with Red Bull since 2012, the aim is to grow the challenge and provide ongoing support to those that successfully complete it, as well as forming an Alumni Club that gives access to special privileges.

- www.riseto.co.uk

Host an event

Invite the press to come and meet you. This doesn't have to be an expensive affair; the secret is partnering with others who could benefit from being in front of your audience. Approach a venue and ask if you can host at no cost, in exchange for the venue receiving profile. Do the same with caterers. Then give invited guests a reason to attend – have a theme, an interesting speaker, a launch announcement, something that will grab their attention and encourage them to attend.

Make use of free online services such as Eventbrite (www.eventbrite.com) or Meetup (www.meetup.com) to send out invites and receive RSVPs.

Attend events

Be seen and heard by getting out and about – a lot!

There's a wealth of events for young start-ups. Most are free or low cost and offer an opportunity to learn from experts, mix with peers, and find new customers and suppliers. To see a full enterprise events listing visit www.startupbritain.org and click on Enterprise Calendar. Activity hots up each November with Global Entrepreneurship Week. Be on the look-out for events happening at your university, college or locally. There's always something going on in StartUp Britain!

- Youth Enterprise Live: 12–13 October | www.youthenterprise-live.co.uk
- Global Entrepreneurship Week: 12–18 November 2012 | www.gew.org.uk

- StartUp Saturday: throughout the year | startupsaturday2012.eventbrite.com
- NACUE events on campus and StartUp Milkround | nacue.com
- StartUp Weekend: hosted in locations across the UK | www.startupweekend.org

Jump On Board!

In October 2012 the StartUp Britain Bus will hit the road and travel to universities and colleges with entrepreneurs and experts on board. They could be coming to your town, bringing free advice on starting a business and people on hand who can help you apply for a loan. Register to receive the StartUp Britain e-news (www.startupbritain.org) and you'll be first to hear about bus tour dates and locations.

Join a society, group or club

Signing up to an enterprise society, a local business club or network is good for business (and your social life). Check out these national business and society networks to find your natural fit:

- 4Networking – national network of business breakfast groups. www.4networking.biz

- Business Scene – hosts regional and national networking events as well as an online directory of over 10,000 events across the UK. www.business-scene.com

- Jelly – casual gatherings of co-workers, with events held in people's homes, the local coffee shop or co-working spaces. The idea is that you meet in relaxed surroundings and creative ideas are stimulated by the experience. www.workatjelly.com

- NACUE – the national organisation that supports and represents student-led enterprise societies and young entrepreneurs in universities and colleges across the UK. www.nacue.com

- The Gazelle Group – 20-plus further education colleges focused on developing entrepreneurial students and environments. www.thegazellegroup.com

- School for Startups – headed by serial entrepreneur Doug Richard, School for Startups travels the UK hosting events for anyone considering starting a business. www.schoolforstartups.co.uk

- Young Entrepreneur Society – founded by young entrepreneur Carly Ward, this is a network that offers education and monthly events to budding business owners. www.youngentrepreneursociety.org.uk

- Intuit 100Up – apply to be part of this group of 100 StartUps and receive access to finance bootcamps and mentoring via a partnership with NACUE. nacue.com/2012/03/introducing-intuit-100up

- Professional Contractors Group (PCG) – if contracting is the life for you, check out the free resources and events hosted by PCG. www.pcg.org.uk

- Virgin Media Pioneers – create a profile and connect with others, plus have the opportunity to pitch to Sir Richard Branson himself via this vibrant network of young entrepreneurs. www.virginmediapioneers.com

- Enterprise Lab – the brainchild of entrepreneurs Ketan Makwana and Naomi Timperley, this organisation hosts events and programmes to equip young people with the skills they need to succeed in business. www.enterpriselab.co.uk

As your business grows, why not offer to go and speak to those younger than you who dream of following in your footsteps? Do so by linking up with:

- National Enterprise Academy – started by *Dragons' Den* entrepreneur Peter Jones, the academy offers a full-time educational course and qualification in enterprise and entrepreneurship for 16–19 year olds. www.pjea.org.uk

- Young Enterprise – a charity that helps 250,000 young people every year to learn more about business. www.young-enterprise.org.uk

- School Speakers – started by entrepreneur and *Apprentice* TV star Claire Young, this organisation matches enterprising and inspiring speakers with schools. www.schoolspeakers.co.uk

BECOME A STARTUP LOCAL CHAMPION: Raise your profile and the likelihood of being approached for talks and coverage in national campaigns by becoming a StartUp Britain Local Champion. As a Local Champ, you'll be the face of StartUp Britain in your area and have opportunities to get involved in projects like High Street StartUp and StartUp Spaces. It's a route to making connections and, best of all, encouraging even more people to become their own boss.

Rajeeb Dey says it's not what you know but who you know that counts. So be sure to network ...

CASE STUDY

NAME: **Rajeeb Dey** | BUSINESS: **Enternships**

Well-known across the UK as a young entrepreneur, Rajeeb Dey's business started as a sideline website whilst he was president of Oxford Entrepreneurs, the society for student entrepreneurs at the University of Oxford. The site was started to provide a useful service to fellow students looking to connect with opportunities in start-ups and small businesses. Now providing the same service but on a much larger scale, Enternships has come a long way in a short time.

"The first version of the site was developed by a university friend who was studying Computer Science," says Rajeeb. "The logo at the time was developed by another friend – actually a medic student! The great thing about starting something whilst studying is that there are a lot of people around you with the skills you need to get going. My family have been supportive from the outset. When I started working on the venture full-time after university I worked from my family home for a while before moving into offices."

The company is now a team of nine people based in offices in Angel, London. Rajeeb secured a first major client in the form of Santander Bank quite early on, and has developed a platform to connect the bank's business customers to students and graduates who are part of the Santander Universities Network (santanderenternships.com).

"To date we've worked with over 4,000 businesses in helping them promote opportunities – the majority of this has been through word of mouth. We've also been fortunate with great media coverage for Enternships in most major newspapers and media outlets. And it's very important to partner with like-minded organisations to help broaden your reach – something I am proactive in doing for Enternships."

The business is now looking overseas for growth, expanding in emerging markets. A local site has been established in South Africa, and other opportunities are being explored with colleges and younger students.

With more enternships comes the prospect of more young start-ups. A good deal for everyone.

- **www.enternships.com** | @enternships

Attend trade shows

Promote your brand by attending the shows your customers attend. Research the best shows by reading industry magazines and visiting online forums where people in your sector are talking.

Trade show tactics

Before the event

Negotiate a good deal – if you're prepared to wait it out, the best deals on stands can be had days before the event is starting. The closer the date, the better the price you'll negotiate as the sales team hurry to get a full house.

Tell people you're going – circulate news that you'll be at the event through online networks (giving your location or stand number) and issue a press release if you're doing something newsworthy at the event, maybe launching a new product, having a guest appearance, running a competition, etc.

At the event

Be clear on the offer – determine what you are selling at the show and let this be consistent across show materials; from pop-up stands to flyers. Be creative with the stand to keep costs low. Pop-up banners can be bought for £45 each from companies like Demonprint (**www.demonprint.co.uk**) and Staples (**www.staples.co.uk**).

Consider offering a supply of mouth-watering refreshments and branded accessories like pens, bags and t-shirts which can be ordered from Vistaprint (**www.vistaprint.co.uk**).

- Collect data – find ways to collect attendees' names and details. Offer a prize in exchange for business cards or take details in exchange for a follow-up information pack or offer. Some events also offer the facility to scan the details from the delegates' badges (for a fee).

- Take friends/family – invite a supportive team. If you're busy talking to a potential customer, you'll want others on the stand who can be doing the same. If there's time, get to know the exhibitors around you.

- Be prepared – wear comfortable shoes, bring some spare clothes and pack your lunch; if you're busy there may not be time to spend buying food and drink!

After the event

- Follow-up – within a couple of days of returning from the show, contact the people who expressed interest so that interest can be turned into sales.

- Plan ahead – if the show delivered a good return, contact the organisers and ask to be considered for a speaking slot or higher profile at the next event, and confirm your willingness to be a case study testimonial story in any post-show promotion.

Jacinta Ingham attends events to build her brand and show off her unique homewares …

CASE STUDY

NAME: **Jacinta Ingham** | BUSINESS: **Whinberry & Antler**

Jacinta Ingham was 24 when she started her hand design and print fabrics business. Whinberry & Antler was the perfect way to create work for herself as a designer after completing a Fine Art degree at Oxford Brookes University in 2010. The company has since grown quickly, becoming well-known for offering unique homeware and soft furnishings in the UK and overseas.

"Whinberry & Antler now sells cushions, lavender bags, aprons, tea towels and draught excluders," says Jacinta. "I'm also in discussion with a ceramics company based in Stoke to create a ceramics range, and upholstering a bespoke hand made wing back armchair frame, which will be covered in Whinberry & Antler fabric. All products are sourced from within the UK."

Jacinta explains that her parents' home-based business was a big influence on her.

"My parents launched IDEA (Ingham Diagnostic Energy Assessors) five years ago from home. Previously to this my father was a secondary school physics teacher and my mother worked for the NHS. Whilst mum still does part-time work for the NHS, my father is employed full-time by IDEA. I would say that their experience in setting up and running a successful business has helped me a great deal in the advice, reassurance and guidance they've given me."

Jacinta has promoted the business mostly online. She started out by selling on Etsy and her own website and now has a store on Folksy, as well as being in the process of joining NotOnTheHighstreet. And international opportunities are opening up, with her products recently made available via Dalani to Sweden, Finland, Poland and Norway.

The next step will be a conversation with UK Trade & Investment about exporting; Jacinta has seen the popularity of her products in America on account of their very British identity.

"The business attended the *Country Living* Spring Fair in London last March. This was more successful than I could have hoped for – a great platform to get the Whinberry & Antler brand out to a wider audience. Through this I have made trade sales, increased my website and blog hits, had direct website sales and the opportunity to have products featured in publications, including a half-price advertorial in *Vogue* magazine."

Jacinta has found that showing people the products in person makes a greater impact than sending images, so the next phase of the marketing plan is to take her products to potential retailers around the UK in person.

- whinberryantler.blogspot.co.uk | @whinberryantler

Become an expert

If you have a special set of knowledge or experience, set yourself up as an expert in your field and the media will come knocking on your door. Here are eight ways in which you can promote your expertise.

1. Publish a book

Become a published author on your special topic. Utilise the book as a business development tool, taking copies to events, and offering free and downloadable versions to potential customers. Being an author lends you credibility and gives customers information and insight. Get in touch with publishers and agents via *The Writer's & Artist's Yearbook*, or self-publish:

- Blurb | www.blurb.com
- Lulu | www.lulu.com
- Ubyu | www.ubyubooks.com

2. Present yourself

Put yourself forward to speak at events (consider asking for a fee and/or costs to be covered) or suggest being a satellite speaker, where you are beamed in via video link-up, so saving the effort and expense of travel. Invite customers and prospects and make the presentation openly available via SlideShare.

- SlideShare.com | www.slideshare.com

3. Host a webinar

Share your expertise or demonstrate a process by hosting a webinar or visual presentation where a live audience can see you and interact. Achieve this via platforms such as GoToMeeting, GoToWebinar and WebEx, and remember to host it at a time that suits your target audience.

- GoToMeeting | www.gotomeeting.com
- GoToWebinar | www.gotomeeting.com/webinar
- WebEx | www.webex.co.uk

4. Produce a film

Maybe the word 'film' is a little ambitious but why not create your own video content and have a sponsored series of guides (or other content) that can be uploaded to video sharing sites such as YouTube, Vimeo and eHow?

- YouTube | www.youtube.com
- Vimeo | www.vimeo.com
- eHow | www.ehow.co.uk

5. Broadcast a podcast

For customers who like to listen to what you have to say at a time that suits them, upload a podcast with top tips, interviews and your thoughts of the day. Make it available on your site, iTunes and Podcast Alley to be sure of a wide audience. Follow the advice below from podcast producer San Sharma on how to record a podcast on a Skype call.

- Submit a podcast to the iTunes store | www.apple.com/itunes/podcasts
- Podcast Alley | www.podcastalley.com

YOU CAN PRODUCE A PODCAST interview using Skype, Pamela Call Recorder, and a little editing know-how. San Sharma shows how it's done, in five simple steps:

1. "Sign up for a free Skype account (www.skype.com) and download the Skype software.

2. "If you're using a Windows machine, download Pamela Call Recorder (www.pamela.biz), which lets you record your Skype calls. If you're on a Mac, you can download Call Recorder for Skype (www.ecamm.com). Both have free

trial versions, but only cost around £13 when that's expired.

3. "Call up your interviewee using Skype. If they're a Skype user, too, that will be a free call but if they're on a fixed or mobile line, you'll need to get some Skype Credit (bit.ly/epymNm)."

4. "Once you've made a connection and agreed with the interviewee the format of the conversation, hit the record button on your call recorder software and you're off!

5. "Edit using Audacity (audacity.sourceforge.net), which is free for Windows and Macs, or with GarageBand (www.apple.com/garageband), which comes with most Macs (you can also buy it as part of the iLife package).

"The easiest way to share your recording is by uploading it to AudioBoo (www.audioboo.com), which lets people listen to it on the web, embedded on your website or via iTunes or a mobile phone."

6. Deliver training

Whether your skill is in embroidering handmade shoes or developing stylish websites, your knowledge could be shared with others. Rather than seeing this as surrendering intelligence to potential competitors, offer instruction you're comfortable with that will create fans and followers who will learn from you, buy from you and, critically, encourage others to do the same. Check out platforms GoToTraining and WebEx, encourage contacts to sign up and then after the demonstration you have a chance to follow up with a group of new contacts.

- GoToTraining | www.gotomeeting.com/fec/training/online_training
- WebEx WebTraining | www.webex.co.uk

7. Develop an app

Take your content and make an iPhone app. Turn to browser-based platforms such as Appmakr; "AppMakr can be used by anyone with existing content and fans or customers to reach; bloggers/writers, business owners, website owners ... ".

You can either set a list price to make sales via the App Store or make it available free of charge.

- AppMakr | www.appmakr.com

8. Form groups

Encourage others to discuss, debate and contribute to your content by forming groups utilising social media platforms such as Facebook, LinkedIn and Ning. Bonding interested people to each other will bond them ever closer to you, the content creator and group host.

- Facebook | www.facebook.com
- LinkedIn | www.linkedin.com
- Ning | www.ning.com

BE EVERYWHERE: Keep in touch with existing customers via a newsletter and reach out to the new by making regular appearances at events, on other people's websites and blogs, in newspapers and magazines, and on radio and TV. Write to the magazines and radio stations that ask people to send in their story. It's a free way to get coverage. The more you're covered, the more you'll be invited to speak and comment, and before you know it, you'll be everywhere!

Price point

These options will raise your profile but you can also generate revenue from them. Your options are:

- make your content and knowledge available at no charge to customers, to build your reputation as the go-to person and place for a particular product or service
- charge for access/downloads/viewing and turn your micropublishing activity into a revenue stream in its own right.

This is something you can assess over time. Start with a mix of charged-for and free content, ensure you're providing good value and incentives for your community to remain interested and engaged, and the options to introduce charged-for content will increase.

Embrace social media

Thanks to social media, there have never been so many tools to promote our businesses free of charge. According to research company Nielsen, the world now spends over 110 billion minutes on social networks and blogs per month. That's 22% of all time online, or one in every four and a half minutes. Embrace this and your business will become known. Here are the key tools to use and, crucially, how best to use them.

Twitter

Visit **www.twitter.com**, create an account, follow friends and contacts (and their followers) and get tweeting.

- **Cost**: free

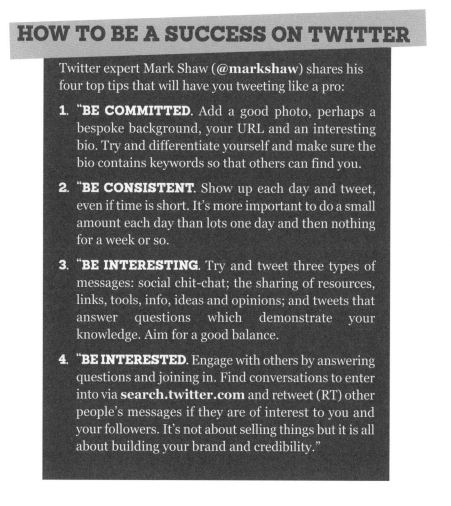

HOW TO BE A SUCCESS ON TWITTER

Twitter expert Mark Shaw (**@markshaw**) shares his four top tips that will have you tweeting like a pro:

1. "**BE COMMITTED**. Add a good photo, perhaps a bespoke background, your URL and an interesting bio. Try and differentiate yourself and make sure the bio contains keywords so that others can find you.

2. "**BE CONSISTENT**. Show up each day and tweet, even if time is short. It's more important to do a small amount each day than lots one day and then nothing for a week or so.

3. "**BE INTERESTING**. Try and tweet three types of messages: social chit-chat; the sharing of resources, links, tools, info, ideas and opinions; and tweets that answer questions which demonstrate your knowledge. Aim for a good balance.

4. "**BE INTERESTED**. Engage with others by answering questions and joining in. Find conversations to enter into via **search.twitter.com** and retweet (RT) other people's messages if they are of interest to you and your followers. It's not about selling things but it is all about building your brand and credibility."

Facebook

Facebook has over 900 million users worldwide, so if you need to be where your customers are, there's a good chance some of them will be there!

You can list on Facebook for free and/or advertise on the site and select target audience based on location, sex, age and interests. As an advertiser, you control how much you want to spend and set a daily budget. The minimum budget is US $1.00 (63p) a day. After designing your ad(s), decide for how long you want the campaign to run and whether you want to be charged for the number of clicks you receive (CPC – charge per click) or the number of times your ad is displayed. Visit www.facebook.com, create an account, invite friends and contacts to join your group and get promoting.

Read how Fraser Smeaton and his business partners have built a successful business on Facebook, download the free eBook *Boost your Business on Facebook* at (www.enterprisenation.com/facebook-book-offer) and visit Social Bizzle (www.socialbizzle.com) to access video tutorials.

- **Cost**: free (ads are charged-for)

CASE STUDY

NAME: **Fraser Smeaton** | BUSINESS: **Morphsuits**

Fraser Smeaton is one of three co-founders of Morphsuits, producers of the all-in-one coloured lycra suit. If you haven't seen it out and about yet, you're likely to soon!

"We started the business in early 2009 after seeing the amazing reaction one of our friends got when he wore a similar suit on a boys' night out. He was like a celebrity, with loads of people buying him drinks and asking for photos."

Recognising a good idea when he saw it, Fraser started a business selling them with his brother and a friend.

"It works very well in that our relationships are strong enough that we can really discuss any issue on its merits without worrying too much about hurting the others' feelings. We had an open discussion when we started that remaining friends was more important than anything else. In the day-to-day running of the business we all have complementary skills which are reflected in our roles."

Gregor is the marketing man, Ali the accountant and Fraser (the one with a commercial background) left to strike deals.

The three co-founders have sourced help from a good many people and organisations, from family members (Fraser's mum now works in the finance department!) to senior people in the companies where they used to work.

"We have always found that you gain an awful lot from discussing your idea and business with as diverse a range of people as possible. You hear quite a lot of silly ideas and misguided criticism, but within that there are some great points that can change your business. The skill is picking out the gems."

When it comes to the role Facebook has played in launching this young business, Fraser is unequivocal:

"Facebook has been a massive help to us. Without it we wouldn't have been able to let people know about our product. The best thing about Facebook is that it allows a good idea to spread very quickly."

When it comes to plans for the next 12 months, Fraser talks about launching more fancy dress brands and a vision to grow into "the Procter & Gamble of fancy dress" – that's quite some vision to have!

- www.morphsuits.co.uk | @morphsuits

TOP TIP: "Test your idea quickly and cheaply. Your idea may look great on paper but you can't be sure it will work until you get going. I had two previous businesses that I still maintain boasted brilliant business plans but we couldn't sell anything. However, we only lost a few hundred pounds and a few months on each, and what we learnt helped us make Morphsuits a success."

LinkedIn

Referring to itself as "the world's largest professional network", LinkedIn has close to 100 million members in over 200 countries. Visit www.linkedin.com, create an account and start connecting with contacts and finding new ones. Form LinkedIn groups around your specialist subject; or, if you are a professional selling creative services, check out the new Creative Portfolio Display application (linkd.in/deDVX1), which aims to "empower creative professionals by creating a one-stop solution for maintaining their work portfolio and broadcasting it to millions".

- **Cost**: free (option to upgrade to a business account, which is a paid-for package)

Flickr

Join **www.flickr.com** and promote yourself visually by uploading photos of you and your products or service, and maybe even a few shots of happy customers. The site also carries video clips so you can show:

- events you host, speak at, or attend
- products you make (the finished product) as well as images of the production process
- happy customers wearing/using/enjoying your products and services
- your workspace
- your family (if you – and they – feel comfortable showing your personal side).

You can also easily pull the photos into your blog and social media pages.

- **Cost**: free (option to upgrade to a pro account which is a paid-for package)

YouTube

YouTube is the world's most popular online video community, with 24 hours of video uploaded every minute. Start your own business channel for free, and upload videos profiling you and your work.

Create an account (**www.youtube.com/create_account**), start a channel (advice via YouTube video!), and start broadcasting to the world. You can give each of your videos a name and assign keywords to it to help with searching, plus you can have a short description of your company on your profile page. Again, these clips are very easy to add to your website, and they help keep the content fresh and interesting.

- **Cost**: free

Pinterest

Pinterest is a virtual pinboard that lets users organise and share the beautiful things they find on the web. Big brands and small businesses have taken to Pinterest to pin pictures of their products to virtual 'pinboards'. More powerfully, customers are pinning their favourite products – and doing some of the marketing work for them!

The site has just over 2 million daily active users. Head to tinyurl.com/ENPinterest to view other Pinteresting facts and figures.

- **Cost:** free

TOTAL BUDGET REQUIRED FOR ONLINE PROMOTION: £0

Measure the results

Time to measure what's working and what's not. Measure media and press mentions through signing up to Google Alerts – and you'll be pleased to know there's a whole host of tools that are free to use and will show real-time results for what's working on your site.

Google Analytics offers intelligence on your website traffic and marketing effectiveness: www.google.com/analytics.

There are other analytics options:

- Alexa – web traffic metrics, site demographics and top URL listings: www.alexa.com

- Clicky – monitors and analyses your site traffic in real time: www.getclicky.com

- Opentracker – gather and analyse web stats and monitor online visitors: www.opentracker.net

- StatCounter – an invisible web tracker and hit counter that offers data in real time: www.statcounter.com

- Marketing Grader – generates a free marketing report that compares your site with a competitor's: www.websitegrader.com

Hopefully what you will see is an upward curve of visitors and time spent on the site.

If you're selling anything, then hopefully this means more sales. If your site is the business, this means you're in a strong position to attract advertisers and begin doing affiliate deals (see page 107).

MONKEYING AROUND: Run a poll with, for example, Wufoo (**www.wufoo.com**) or Survey Monkey (**www.surveymonkey.com**). Both are free to use, then publish the results via a press release and online. The media loves good polls!

Look out, in particular, for the sources of your traffic (which are your highest referring sites) and your most popular pages. You can see days where your site receives spikes in visitor levels (and track this back to marketing) and measure if visitors are spending longer periods on the site and which times are popular, e.g. weekends, evenings, lunchtimes, etc.

Use the following template to ensure you're making the most of all your marketing opportunities.

Template 7: Marketing and Promotion

Media

Press (local and national)

List relevant names and journalists

Radio

List programmes on which you'd like to appear

Television

List programmes on which you'd like to appear

Magazines

List target titles

Online

List target sites

Other

Events

List events to attend; networking and trade. What about hosting your own event, too?

Awards

List awards relevant to your business and their dates of entry

Your social network

Plan of action for engaging with major social networks on ongoing basis

III. GROW

With marketing and sales underway, you are getting known and making money. Now it's time to grow your profits by outsourcing, keeping the business in balance, staying on top of cash flow and getting some good support.

66 Write your own rules –
whilst you shouldn't
ignore advice from other
successful entrepreneurs,
don't be a slave to their
methods. You know your
business best and can
navigate your own way. **99**

– Jess Butcher,
founder, Blippar

13. ATTRACT CUSTOMERS BACK

You are making sales via your site and developing a strong community of fans and followers. Give visitors and customers a reason to return with content that is regularly updated.

If you have a blog, try to post regularly, and if you're selling, keep the product range updated. Give your site some TLC each day, as fresh content will attract visitors who want to see what's new and will also appeal to the trawling web spiders who determine search engine results.

User-generated content

Encourage your site visitors to get to know each other through a forum or comment boxes. Before you know it, a sense of community will develop and visitors will log on each day to find out who's saying what and what's happening with whom.

Exclusive offers

Extend offers to your existing customers, readers or members that will tempt them back. This offer could be conditional on customers referring a friend: that way your customer returns to the site with others in tow. Add to this with a badge of honour; design an icon that visitors can display on their own site to show their affiliation with you.

Guest appearances

Invite special guests to appear on your site via guest blog posts, hosting a webchat or a featured interview.

Keep in touch

Communicate all these good and sticky things to your users through a regular e-newsletter powered by sites such as MailChimp (www.mailchimp.com), Constant Contact (www.constantcontact.com) or AWeber Communications (www.aweber.com).

Email marketing: keep it clean, keep it simple, keep it relevant

Email marketing works best when it is targeted. This means keeping your lists clean and organising them according to previous customer contact. A well-segmented list means you can send more frequent campaigns, ensuring a steady flow of business, without worrying about clogging up inboxes. Keep your email designs clean and simple – making it easier for your customer to make informed buying decisions in a snap.

14. FOCUS ON WHAT YOU DO BEST AND OUTSOURCE THE REST

The business is growing, time is your most precious resource and you are in need of help. The quickest and most affordable place to get it is from other companies with whom you can partner to get projects done, as well as from expert advisors and mentors who will offer advice on how the business can continue to grow.

With outsourcing you can free yourself up to dedicate your attention to sales, strategy or whatever the business activity is that you do best. My advice to all businesses is always: *focus on what you do best and outsource the rest*.

What can be outsourced and to whom?

Admin

Hire a VA (virtual assistant) to do the admin tasks you don't want or don't have the time to do:

- International Association of Virtual Assistants | www.iava.co.uk
- Society of Virtual Assistants | www.societyofvirtualassistants.co.uk
- VA Success Group | www.vasuccessgroup.co.uk
- Virtual Assistant Coaching & Training Company | www.vact.co.uk
- Virtual Assistant Forums | www.virtualassistantforums.com

Accounts

Unless you are in the accountancy business, this is almost a must to be outsourced. Monthly payroll, accounts, VAT returns and corporate tax returns all take time and it's time you can't afford or simply don't have. A cost/benefit analysis is likely to show that it's cheaper to outsource to a qualified accountant. Ask around for recommendations of accountants in your area who deliver a quality service at a competitive cost and are registered with the Institute of Chartered Accountants for England and Wales.

For online accounting and invoicing that makes life easier for you and your accountant, check out:

- FreeAgent | www.freeagentcentral.com
- KashFlow | www.kashflow.co.uk
- QuickBooks | www.quickbooks.co.uk

IN THE KIT

Meet all your accounting software needs with deals from FreeAgent, KashFlow and QuickBooks from Intuit.

PR, marketing and design

Outsource your PR to a specialist who can be pitching and promoting the business whilst you're at work. Find skilled professionals on directory sites such as Enterprise Nation (www.enterprisenation.com), Elance (www.elance.com) and PeoplePerHour (www.peopleperhour.com).

Sales

Hire a sales expert to make calls, set up appointments and attend trade shows. Find these professionals online, contact telemarketing companies that offer outbound sales calls as a service, or look at sales specialists such as Winning Sales (www.winningsales.co.uk).

Customer service

Looking after customers is vital, but even that can be outsourced. Get Satisfaction's tagline is "people-powered customer service" – it provides a web-hosted platform, much like a forum, where customers can ask questions, suggest improvements, report a problem or give praise. It can save you time and money by having the power of the crowd take care of customer questions!

- Get Satisfaction | www.getsatisfaction.com

IT

Spending too many hours trying to fix a single IT problem? Outsource the hassle and save your time, money and blood pressure. Find IT professionals online or contact IT support teams connected to the large retailers.

- Geeks-on-Wheels | www.geeks-on-wheels.com
- Knowhow | www.knowhow.com
- Geek Squad | www.geeksquad.co.uk

In launching and growing her business, Charlie Ashworth understands the value of focusing on her strengths and bringing in experts to help in other areas ...

CASE STUDY

NAME: Charlie Ashworth | **BUSINESS**: Venture Proof

Charlie Ashworth's entrepreneurial career started when she became a freelance toy inventor. She's now boss of Venture Proof, a consultancy practice offering intellectual property advice to small business owners.

"I graduated in industrial design and technology and went to work for one of the UK's leading product design consultancies. We used to have product brainstorms with experts from different industries, and one day in walked a bunch of toy inventors. Having been a fan of *Big*, the Tom Hanks film [in which an eight-year-old boy is transformed overnight into an adult and flourishes as a toy inventor in New York], I couldn't help but ask them how they got involved in such an exciting industry. They had the dream job, and I wanted to be part of it. I was very lucky that they offered to take a look at my toy ideas. Before you know it, I had become part of the team. The day I walked past my first licensed toy invention on the shelves in Hamleys, Regent Street, was a great one!"

Charlie then moved from inventing toys to advising on patents. In spending time on patent searching, Charlie discovered an interest in intellectual property and wanted to learn more about the area. The company supported Charlie through a master's degree in IP law and management, which offered a good grounding in the different types of IP, and from there her interest grew.

"I still see myself as a toy inventor," she says. Just last month she managed to license another product. But "having the knowledge to protect ideas seemed to be getting more and more important to my line of work so I decided to take the next step and train to become a patent attorney. I'm now a Chartered UK and European patent attorney, with my own firm. I started it to offer a fresh approach to IP protection for entrepreneurs and people with great ideas."

Going for growth

"I very swiftly realised you can't do everything yourself," says Charlie, "and that by concentrating on the bits you're good at, and finding others to cover the rest, makes for a more efficient and effective business. I have two business mentors who are an amazing sounding board for ideas. They help me keep the business on track. They have a wealth of experience between them, and tapping into that knowledge has boosted both my confidence and profits!"

Charlie is confident she's spotted a gap in the market for a fresh approach to IP and is keen to encourage people to protect their ideas; be it a brand name by a trademark, or new product ideas through patents and registered designs.

With mentors on side and experts on call, this toy inventor and IP advisor looks in good shape to succeed.

- **www.ventureproof.com** | @ventureproof

TOP TIP: "Don't try to do everything yourself. Spot where you need help, and find someone to take care of it, leaving you to concentrate on where you can add real value."

Steps to successful outsourcing

Do the groundwork

Spend some time working on the task yourself so you've built foundations before handing it over to someone else. For example, if you outsource sales then have a ready-made contacts list and some open doors that the specialist can build on, rather than starting from scratch. This will make it more cost-effective for you and means that they hit the ground running.

Be clear on the brief

Having spent some time doing the task yourself, you will have a clear idea of the brief. Back to the example of outsourcing sales, if you've spent 6–12 months sourcing leads and making contacts, you'll have a much clearer idea of the type of work the specialist should do.

The clearer the brief, the better the results.

Take your time

And take references. Spend time evaluating the specialists in the market and, if you can, talk to their existing clients. Do they have the industry experience you're after? Will they represent your brand in a professional manner? Have they delivered a good job for other clients? When an outsourced arrangement works well, the partner becomes part of your team – so choose them as carefully as you would choose an employee.

Let go!

Outsourcing means having to let go a little. Someone else becomes accountable for these results. Embrace this rather than resist it. As the business owner you remain in ultimate control but the expert will need their own space in which to flourish. Outsourcing can save you time and help make you money. Finding the right partner, on the right terms, will make you feel like a new and liberated person.

Form teams

Once you've chosen your outsourced partner(s), it's important to keep in regular contact and work together as a team. There are a number of online project management and collaboration tools to help you stay on top of projects and in control of the company.

Basecamp

Basecamp is the project management tool we rely on at Enterprise Nation. This is a top-class product that allows you to create projects, invite people to view them, upload files and make comments. It's effective online project management that can be accessed from anywhere.

- www.basecamp.com

Google Docs

Share documents via Google Docs. You can edit on the move, choose who accesses documents and share changes in real time.

- docs.google.com

Huddle

Offers simple and secure online workspaces. Huddle is hosted, so there's no software to download and it's free to get started.

- www.huddle.com

Solutions to enable group-talk

- GoToMeeting | www.gotomeeting.com

Work with anyone, anywhere with this easy to use online meeting tool.

- Ketchup | www.useketchup.com

Share and record meeting notes.

- Powwownow | www.powwownow.co.uk

Free conference calling at 'open access' level. Priced packages available.

Form partnerships

If relationships develop, you may decide to form a partnership. Consider writing a partnership agreement as your pre-nup in business. At the outset of a relationship, all is good and you're excited about the potential, but it's best to be safe; have the terms written and agreed so that all parties are clear on expectations.

The following should not be taken as concrete legal advice, more of a guideline on how to draw up an agreement.

Scope of agreement

What is your partnership working to achieve? For example, "This agreement is made between Company A and Company B. The agreement is related to the generation of online advertising revenues/hosting of an event/development of a new product."

Respective responsibilities

Set out the expectations on who does what. For example, Company A will be responsible for promotion and business development and Company B will take on technical development and client care. Also include a note of how you'll keep each other briefed, maybe through the use of an online project management tool.

Finances

What will be the split in revenue, and is this before or after costs? And who owns the intellectual property of the product/service/activity? Consider including a clause that states the agreement will be reviewed in six months so that both parties can check on progress and have the right to cease the agreement if it hasn't gone as planned.

Be fair

Agreements where both parties feel that they're receiving their fair share are likely to be longer-lasting than those when one party feels embittered. Talk about this before writing and concluding the agreement. Make sure there's no resentment or sense of being exploited on either side.

Sign it!

After making the effort to produce an agreement, be sure to sign it! And then store it so that you can access it easily if the need arises.

When writing the clauses in your agreement, think about all the things that could go wrong and safeguard against them. It's a practical exercise and won't harm your newly formed business relationship but will get it off on a firm footing. If you're looking for a template agreement, check out sites such as www.clickdocs.co.uk.

BUSINESS OWNER PLUS ONE: When the business is at a stage to take on its first new employee, visit the Taking on an Employee section of the Business Link site (**tinyurl.com/takingonanemployee**), which offers details on how to employ and your obligations as an employer over time.

15. KEEP THE BUSINESS IN BALANCE

As the business continues to grow, you will want to maintain momentum and grow at a comfortable pace. Achieve this by following what I call 'the golden triangle', which will keep you and the business in balance. This requires spending roughly a third of your time on three key things:

1. Customer care

Look after your customers by delivering a quality product or service, on time and within budget. And remember … the customer is always right!

I ask clients for feedback so that I can keep a check on what they're thinking and changes they'd like to see. It's good to know some personal details about your customers, too. (Maybe their birthday, their favourite hobby.) As you gather these details, make a quick note so you can send a birthday card on the right date, etc. Don't go overboard, but showing that you care certainly won't harm your relationship.

Offer customers good service, regular communication and an innovative line of products and services. It will stand you in good stead.

2. New business

Taking care of customers means taking care of sales. Why? Because it costs less to win business from existing customers than it does to find new ones. If customers are happy, they'll say good things about you to new and potential customers. This is called word-of-mouth marketing and achieving it is every business owner's dream!

Secure new clients through marketing, encouraging recommendations, and direct-sales calls and pitches.

3. Admin

Not as enjoyable as the first two, but it still has to be done. Keep the books in order by raising invoices in good time, being on top of cash flow, and filing tax returns and company documents on time and in order. In short, keep the finances in check and the books up-to-date.

Cash is king

In Chapter 9 we looked at the topic of straightforward finance and how to plan income and outgoings.

Keep an eye on the accounts so you can see how much money is in the bank, how much is owed and whether this covers your outgoings.

This is a vital part of running your business and something you will need to keep close tabs on especially at the start. Monitor this using your accounts software and online banking. It's a very well worn phrase in business, but cash is most definitely king - without it your business won't work - no matter how hard you do!

Getting paid and paying others

A key part in managing your cash flow is making sure you get paid and get paid promptly. How you get paid will depend quite a lot on the type of business you have and whether you are selling direct to customers or to other businesses. If selling directly, you will mostly be paid immediately. If you are dealing with other businesses, the chances are most will expect to pay on invoice (more on this below) and will expect a credit period in which to pay. Be prepared to offer credit terms, but be careful about how long you give, how much credit you'll allow and who you offer this to.

If you need to buy in products or services from others as part of your business it's always worth seeing if you too can arrange credit terms with suppliers. This should help you balance payments in and out. This isn't always easy at the start and you may have to pay upfront to begin with, but it is something to ask for. Having built up a good relationship with your supplier it should be a natural next step.

Invoices

Be on time with invoicing and keep a record of amounts outstanding. I have a simple spreadsheet with five columns labelled 'client', 'invoice amount', 'invoice number', 'date submitted' and 'date paid'.

- Your invoices should be a simple document with basic details. The less cause for question on the invoice, the faster it will be paid.

- Always find out in advance who should be named on the invoice, where it should be sent and whether you need to include any sort of order reference number. When dealing with large companies in particular, this sort of thing can make a big difference to how quickly you get paid.

- Settle invoices as promptly as you can. Your suppliers should be grateful and repay you with good service.

See the next page for an example invoice.

Hopefully your clients and customers will always pay promptly, but occasionally you might need to remind them. Do this politely and clearly. It's often sensible to send a monthly statement to a client detailing any outstanding invoices, and usually that's enough to spur them into action.

You can balance the budget with a piece of accounting software. See 'Accounts' on page 144 for details of options, and don't forget to have a look at the offers available in this kit.

Receipts

Keep business-related receipts in a place where they're easy to find. I have a big wicker box that I use as a collecting place for receipts. It's helpful that they're all in one place when it's time to do the VAT return.

Track your time with time-tracking software

- Cashboard | www.getcashboard.com

- Four Four Time | www.fourfourtime.co.uk

- TraxTime | www.spudcity.com/traxtime

SAMPLE INVOICE

1. Name of your contact

2. The date

3. An address to which the cheque shall be sent or bank details for accounts in which monies should be deposited

4. Company registration and VAT number (if applicable)

5. Invoice number and client's purchase order (PO) number

6. Payment terms (e.g. payable within 30 days of receipt), and by cheque, transfer, etc.

7. A brief product description or summary of services

8. Amount owing (inclusive or exclusive of VAT, depending on whether you're registered).

I think it's good practice to include a cover note, too, that confirms what's being invoiced and thanks the client for their custom.

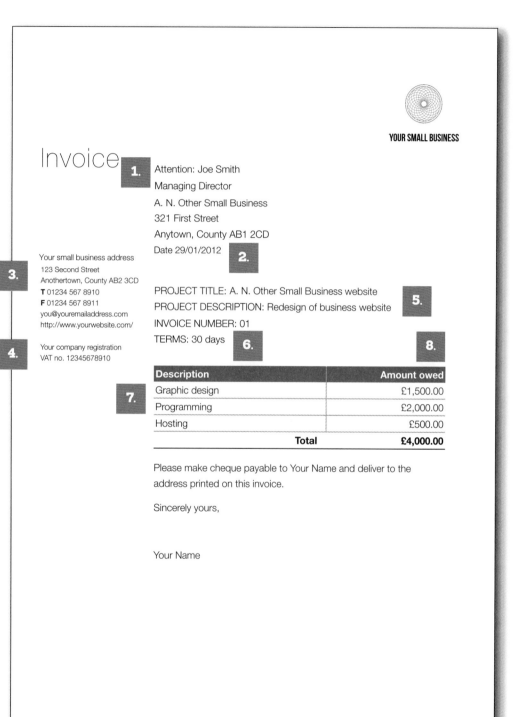

Invoice **1.**

Attention: Joe Smith
Managing Director
A. N. Other Small Business
321 First Street
Anytown, County AB1 2CD
Date 29/01/2012 **2.**

Your small business address
123 Second Street
Anothertown, County AB2 3CD
T 01234 567 8910
F 01234 567 8911
you@youremailaddress.com
http://www.yourwebsite.com/

3.

Your company registration
VAT no. 12345678910

4.

PROJECT TITLE: A. N. Other Small Business website
PROJECT DESCRIPTION: Redesign of business website
INVOICE NUMBER: 01
TERMS: 30 days **6.**

5.

8.

7.

Description	Amount owed
Graphic design	£1,500.00
Programming	£2,000.00
Hosting	£500.00
Total	**£4,000.00**

Please make cheque payable to Your Name and deliver to the address printed on this invoice.

Sincerely yours,

Your Name

YOUR SMALL BUSINESS

16. SUPPORT

All of the success stories in this kit have spoken of the valuable support received from friends, family, advisors and experienced entrepreneurs. And in receiving your StartUp Loan, you'll be offered business support as an additional part of the package.

Ask questions at every opportunity and build a support network. Here's where to look for people who are happy to help.

Peers

Who better to turn to than those going through the same experience as you? Visit the sites below and join their active communities of business owners.

- Enterprise Nation | www.enterprisenation.com
- Business Zone | www.businesszone.co.uk
- Start Up Donut | www.startupdonut.co.uk
- Smarta | www.smarta.com
- Startups | startups.co.uk
- Fresh Business Thinking | www.freshbusinessthinking.com
- School for Startups | www.schoolforstartups.co.uk

Nathan Bestwick has seen firsthand the benefits of support and mentors for his business ...

CASE STUDY

NAME: **Nathan Bestwick** | **BUSINESS**: **Yormii**

Product designer Nathan Bestwick started his
first business – If? Works – in 2007, aged 22.
He's now launched a second, Yormii, with
backing from investors. Nathan's close to
finishing work on Yormii's first product – an
innovative pepper mill that will hit the shops in
early 2013.

"I won the Sheffield Hallam University award for
enterprise and innovation in 2010, which got the
attention of Gripple, a local manufacturing
company. They run Incub which helps young
entrepreneurs with intellectual property to
develop their product and get it to market.

"Gripple put money into the new business in
return for equity and I contributed the intellectual
property. We got some money from banks as well, but it's nowhere near as much as I
need, so I had to invest a chunk of my own money and find another partner.

"It's actually worked out incredibly well," says Nathan. He found someone through a
family friend who makes marinades and spices and sells them to large retailers. Having
complementary products meant that, even though it dilutes his shareholding, he has a
partner who can get his products into big retailers straightaway.

And when it comes to the product, Nathan is something of a perfectionist:

"I've spent a long time just trying to get the product right and it's been through ten or
15 versions. The Millmii is a pepper mill that you rub between your hands. It doesn't
require any gripping or twisting so it's very good for people with arthritis. But it also
has huge appeal for young professionals who want colourful and innovative products."

Meanwhile, "Gripple have given me a lot of support and I've been using their computer-
aided design systems. I've had to learn new software and how to engineer a product
that can be manufactured for the market."

Nathan has also had to run the business on top of that. That meant "a huge volume of
things" he had to learn. "I had to develop prototypes to show to buyers and then go out
on the road and become a salesman. I'm not a natural salesman! There's also been the
business planning side of it: thinking ahead, factoring in cash flow, and pitching to
banks."

Nathan even flew out to China for 48 hours to speak to potential manufacturers. "That was a very easy decision," he says, "because one of them specialises in the plastics I'm using and already makes products for the same market. I visited their factory to make sure it met the standards I required and negotiated the price. We're currently waiting on stock."

Finding support

Through all this, where has Nathan found support? "My mum ran a petrol station for 40 years," he explains, "which my grandfather built from scratch with his own hands. They've been a huge inspiration to me. I've also had several mentors in the past four years which has meant I've had someone to ask questions of and to point me in the right direction. They're mostly people I came across at business networking events, but my current mentor works at Gripple, so that's perfect."

- www.yormii.com | www.facebook.com/YormiiUK | @yormii

TOP TIP: "Ask as many people as possible about anything you need at the time. But don't trust the first person you come to, either – it's about knowing what you want and not going into what other people want. I've had my moments of naivety, but it's my business at the end of the day."

Mentors

If you haven't been introduced to a mentor as part of your StartUp Loan, find one via Mentorsme.co.uk, and when you're ready to become a mentor yourself, get trained up as part of the Get Mentoring programme (getmentoring.org).

And don't restrict yourself to one mentor! I have learnt from many people as my businesses have passed through different stages of development. My approach was to get in touch with the person I felt best placed to have the answer, take on board their views, consider my options, and then act.

In my view, the ideal mentor is someone who possesses four things:

1. experience of your industry/sector
2. the ability to listen
3. the technical skills to advise
4. a willingness to make introductions to useful contacts.

If you can find these in one person, you are very fortunate indeed.

One of the finest things a mentor can do is allow you to talk. By doing so, you often work out the answer. Sometimes you just need an experienced sounding board.

Business advisors

Consider approaching your local enterprise agency, university/college society, chamber of commerce or the Prince's Trust for additional support.

- National Enterprise Network (www.nationalenterprisenetwork.org) offers links to local business support agencies in your area

- NACUE (www.nacue.org) represents enterprise societies in universities and colleges that could be your first port of call.

- In 2011, the Prince's Trust (tinyurl.com/princestrustenterprise) helped almost 13,000 young people through its Enterprise Programme. Through involvement with the StartUp Loans programme, this figure is expected to be higher still for 2012 and beyond.

- Local Enterprise Partnerships (www.bis.gov.uk/policies/economic-development/leps) have been set up to encourage enterprise and will be interested in hearing any success story.

- British Chambers of Commerce (www.britishchambers.org.uk) offer specific services relating to export. Some have Junior Chambers for younger members.

It was thanks to The Prince's Trust that Jide Johnson-Babatunde was able to get into business ...

CASE STUDY

NAME: **Jide Johnson-Babatunde** |
BUSINESS: **Aniboxx**

Digital animator Jide Johnson-Babatunde started working for himself aged 24 in 2009. In 2011 he formed Aniboxx with a friend from college and now runs a growing business creating animated viral marketing campaigns for other companies.

"I've been drawing since I was six," says Jide. "I've always been interested in art and studied design and technology at college. I was going to be an engineer or architect or other things that my family wanted me to be. But I studied 3D animation at the University of Hertfordshire and loved every minute of it.

"I worked in the industry for a year, but the company couldn't offer me a permanent job because of the recession. I'd seen how things worked, so I decided to do something for myself. I worked as a freelancer to support myself – initially from home then from a small office in Tottenham.

"I'm very well networked and started meeting other young entrepreneurs who were interested in having animated videos to explain their product and get their message across and I realised there was an opportunity. What really helped me get off the ground was getting my business partner, Tunde Omodara, involved. Tunde's a friend from college who's run his own factory for ten years and he always said we'd do something together."

The two formed Aniboxx, with Tunde putting in some of his own money and helping Jide to get start-up funding from The Prince's Trust and Shell LiveWIRE. They then moved into an office in Clerkenwell, "where there are a lot more opportunities to network with likeminded people". Jide has been freelancing work out to other animators and is about to take on his first full-time employee, a PA and business development officer.

The importance of getting the right support

"I'm not one of these people who was selling sweets in school – I was drawing murals. So it's been a huge learning curve to get my head around how business works. Tunde has more business experience and we have complementary skills. He concentrates on growth strategy while I focus on perfecting the product. But I'm also making the conversion to meeting clients and making sales – and we've already picked up Google as a client.

"I also have a mentor through The Prince's Trust and he's the person I'm accountable to. He's only a year older than me, but he's already set up a successful law firm. At first we spoke every week or two, but now I try to talk to him two or three times a week. It's not that I want to be spoon-fed, but I want him to know the moves that are being made so I can move a bit more quickly and he can help me become a better decision maker.

"There's a lot of personal development involved, because so much of the business is the person who started it. If I go left, the business goes left. If I go right, the business goes right. I have to think about how I move and manage the finances and the direction of the company. I'm trying to get a helicopter view of the company and I'm feeling more like I can run the operation, provided I have the right skills on board."

- www.aniboxx.com | www.facebook.com/Aniboxx | @Aniboxx

Accelerate!

And finally ... if you want to give your business an extra injection and growth spurt, check out some of the 'Accelerators' launched by companies to give you space, funding and access to technology and customers.

- Wayra | www.wayra.org/en/wayra-uk-2012
- School for Creative Startups | www.schoolforcreativestartups.com
- Iris Ventures | www.irisnation.com/irisnews/uk_europe/iris-launches-business-incubator-iris-ventures
- Accelerator Academy | www.acceleratoracademy.com
- New Entrepreneurs Foundation | www.newentrepreneursfoundation.co.uk
- Entrepreneur First | www.entrepreneurfirst.org.uk
- Springboard | www.springboard.com
- Microsoft BizSpark | www.microsoft.com/BizSpark

CASE STUDY

NAME: Oliver Bridge | **BUSINESS**: Currently employed

Oliver Bridge was seven when he first started out in business. He's been busy ever since and sees self-employment as an ideal route to pick up the skills you need to also be a popular employee!

"A friend and I used to make a magazine, photocopy it on my dad's printer and sell it to our neighbours when I was about seven – it was called StarBest and had crosswords and stories about local pets and stuff. Sales struggled to be honest and it only survived to two issues!

"When I was 12 I started a mobile disco with another friend and that was much more successful – we used to do weddings, 21st birthday parties and kids' discos and made a healthy living out of it. We used to reinvest the profits into buying more kit which meant we built up a good show with top lights and speakers etc. so our prices kept going up!

"I started biggerfeet.com when I was 15 because I couldn't find big enough shoes for my size-13 feet. I built the website myself in the summer between my GCSEs and when I launched, found myself on BBC Breakfast, CNN and in the *Financial Times*. I sold shoes worldwide and to all sorts of people – from chemical companies to transvestites!"

Whilst applying to Oxford University, Oliver sold the company to his mum and brother as he wanted to devote his three years of university to his degree ... and to having a social life. Selling to family was a natural move as they had been involved from the start.

"A friend of my mum (and now her fiancée!) helped me with a start-up cash float for biggerfeet.com as well as helping me through all the legal and regulatory bits of starting a company which aren't actually that difficult, but nonetheless daunting when you're 15! I also employed my mum and my brother to help me with wrapping shoes and helping customers, and then ultimately sold it to them – there is no way I could have built the business without them."

The business is still going strong and, after graduation, Oliver decided to take a job with an innovation agency called Happen, working with brands including Bacardi, HSBC and Strepsils to create new products and campaigns.

"I spent a lot of time talking to consumers and turning what they say into new ideas. It was such a fascinating experience – learning how to translate needs into actual products for some of the world's biggest brands."

After a year at Happen, Oliver decided it was time to be closer to entrepreneurs and joined private equity firm Synova Capital. At Synova, Oliver is responsible for speaking to entrepreneurs and identifying businesses in which the fund can invest

"Having the opportunity to meet inspirational people and help them take their businesses to the next level is very rewarding. I get to work alongside some incredibly impressive entrepreneurs and see how businesses are created first-hand."

When asked whether running a business gave him the skills to be useful in the workplace, Oliver replies:

"Absolutely – thanks to my business adventures in my younger years I have a much better understanding of accounts, cash flow problems and how things should be priced – all of which are very useful. It has also helped because it forced me to talk to adults whilst I was still young and I think that gives you a good foundation for handling difficult conversations with customers and colleagues which are inevitable at some point in the workplace!"

This young entrepreneur may be in the workplace for now but expect to see him back at the helm of his own business in years to come!

TOP TIP: "Get out and speak to your customers about your idea. If they like it, great –make it and sell it to them! If they don't like it, keep changing it until they do, and then you're set!"

THE BEST OF LUCK

You've read the stories, devoured the tips and completed the templates. It's time to put that StartUp Loan to work and get the business up and running.

I hope what you've picked up from this kit is that if you're young and starting out as your own boss, there's support all around. In whichever direction you turn, you'll find people to cheer you along and answer your questions.

Make the most of the support on offer and never be afraid to seek help or approach mentors. With guidance from those who've trodden the entrepreneurial path, you will find your own way and build a future that offers financial reward and freedom in your working life.

With thanks to Lord Young who spotted the gap in the market for funding and devised StartUp Loans in response. He's likely to be thanked by thousands of businesses to come!

Best wishes to James Caan and the board of the StartUp Loans Company as they build this important project into a key element of economic recovery for the UK.

And very best wishes to you as you embark on your business journey and what's sure to be an exciting adventure!

EMMA JONES | @EMMALJONES

Turn to Twitter for business tips, advice and banter! These tweeps are worth a follow ...

50 TWEEPS TO FOLLOW

@alexdmitchell
@bipc
@bisgovuk
@BradBurton
@BusinessZone
@carlyyes
@ClaireLYoung
@Dan_Martin
@dickpalmerccn
@dougrichard
@dragonjones
@duncanbannatyne
@e_nation
@emmaljones
@EnCountry
@enternships
@enterpriselabuk
@EntreFirst
@glasses_jamie
@hmrcgovuk
@hushpreet
@iamstartacus
@inspirenetNE
@jamescaan
@Ketan_Makwana

@lordlancaster
@LukeJohnsonRCP
@mattTP
@NACUE
@nacuecreate
@naomitimperley
@OliBarrett
@princestrust
@Rajdey
@sevenhillsviews
@shaawasmund
@smartahq
@startupsfeed
@startupdonut
@Stujbanderson
@shelllivewireuk
@startupbritain
@TheoPathitis
@TheLordYoung
@ukmarketinghelp
@vmpioneers
@nesta_uk
@yenterpriselive
@youngenterprise
@youngstapreneur

WITH THANKS

To the following people who have contributed their expertise, story or tip in the compilation of this kit:

The young entrepreneurs

Maria Allen | **Maria Allen Jewellery**

Beckie Andrews | **Not for Ponies**

Charlie Ashworth | **Venture Proof**

Jide Johnson-Babatunde | **Aniboxx**

Nathan Bestwick | **Yormii**

Oliver Bridge | **Biggerfeet.com**

Richard Brigg | **Usborne Books**

Rajeeb Dey | **Enternships**

James Eder | **The Beans Group**

Jermaine Hagan & Dennis Owusu-Sem | **Revision App**

Cha Haxell | **Large Cup Lingerie**

Rich Hewitt | **SpinCycle**

Richard Hurtley | **Rampant Sporting**

Jacinta Ingham | **Whinberry & Antler**

Katie Leamon | **Katie Leamon**

Lauren Moulsley | **Avon**

Fraser Smeaton | **Morphsuits**

Katie Smith | **Tastes Marvellous**

Zac Williams | **GradTouch**

David Young | **Yang Li Feng**

Inspiring quotes

Michael Acton-Smith | **founder, Moshi Monsters**

Jess Butcher | **co-founder, Blippar**

Melody Hossaini | **CEO, InspirEngage International**

Luke Johsnon | **Chairman, Risk Capital Partners**

Claire Young | **founder, School Speakers**

Experts

Emily Coltman | **FreeAgent**

John Hayes | **iContact**

Laura Rigney | **Pitcher House**

Mark Shaw | **Twitter expert**

Greg Simpson | **Press For Attention**

Jackie Wade | **Winning Sales**

Dan Wilson | **Tamebay**

Joanna Tall | **Off To See My Lawyer**

Andy Yates | **Angel investor**

Enterprise Nation

Simon Wicks

San Sharma

Myles Hunt

Louise Hinchen

Chris Read

Chris Parker

BIS Team

Nichola Bruno

Greg Chammings

Tom Clementson

Paul Lewis

Ellie Mond

IV. OFFERS & PARTNERS

HOW TO ACCESS YOUR OFFERS

To take advantage of the offers detailed in this section, head to:

www.enterprisenation.com/slk

Enter the code below, select the individual offers you want, and you'll be shown the links and offer codes you need.

You don't have to access all the offers at once if you don't want to; you can come back at any time.

We'll be adding new offers throughout the year and you'll be able to access those too.

ACCESS CODE: slk0512

A SUIT THAT FITS

Looking the part while you set up your business is very important. That's why A Suit That Fits are extending this great offer:

A bespoke two-piece suit for £209* from the professional range, or if you get swayed by one of their luxury cloths in the distinguished or premiere ranges they'll give you £50* off your order.

A bit about A Suit That Fits

A Suit That Fits create bespoke, ethically hand-tailored suits for men and women. With over 30 locations nationwide and a team of expert Style Advisors, they're tailoring the nation one stitch at a time.

The business began as a start-up just like yours six years ago, when founders Warren Bennett and David Hathiramani revolutionised how tailoring could be done – streamlining the process so that everybody could create stunning suits that fit them at accessible prices. Now A Suit That Fits creates more suits a week than the whole of Saville Row put together, and allows men and women to create their very own bespoke creations from 40 billion style combinations.

www.asuitthatfits.com

*Terms and Conditions apply – please visit www.aSuitThatFits.com/termsandconditions for more information

Protect your new business with AXA business insurance

Securing funding is really important – especially if you're just starting out. But what if you make a mistake or someone is injured as a result of what you do? You might be sued, which could ground your business before it even takes off.

Business insurance will give you the right protection – as well as peace of mind.

- If you provide a service or give advice, professional indemnity insurance will protect your business if you make a mistake or are negligent.

- If there's risk of damage, loss or injury at your place of work – whether it's your office or your customer's home – public liability insurance will cover you in the event of a claim.

- And when you decide to employ extra help – you'll need employers' liability insurance. It's the law.

Remember, nowadays even minor incidents can lead to major claims for compensation.

That's why AXA Business Insurance is bringing you an exclusive offer. Get a quote online today and get one months' free cover – on top of the 10% discount we give you for buying online.

business.axainsurance.com

Terms and conditions

One month's free cover, which is given by an 8.5% discount from the annual premium applies only to AXA business insurance policies (non motor classes) bought direct from AXA through business.axainsurance.com and is valid for quotes dated between 28 May and 30 November 2012. Quotations and cover cannot be guaranteed as some trades/risks may not be acceptable to AXA Insurance underwriters and all quotations are subject to AXA standard terms, conditions, limitations and exclusions. The premium can be paid as one annual payment or evenly split across 10 monthly instalments.
Customers must be claims free.
Quotations are valid for 30 days from the date quotation is given. All quotations are subject to policy minimum premiums which override any discounts and take precedence.
This offer is not available to existing AXA business insurance policyholders.
This discount is in addition to the 10% online discount available to customers who complete the purchase of their business insurance online at business.axainsurance.com/get-quote.
All insurance is arranged, underwritten and administered by AXA Insurance UK plc, a member of the AXA Group of Companies who are authorised and regulated by the Financial Services Authority.
Registered in England No: 78950. Registered Office : 5 Old Broad Street, London, EC2N 1AD. Telephone calls may be monitored or recorded.

Founded in 2000 with one site, Bizspace has now been providing flexible, affordable business accommodation to both the SME and corporate markets for 12 years and has grown to 110 locations in both England and Scotland.

Bizspace provides the easiest, most flexible and cost-effective way to occupy business premises in the UK.

Finding ideal business premises for your organisation can be difficult, but with over 7m sq ft on 110 sites, Bizspace will be able to provide the right commercial units, offices, studio space, industrial premises or simple storage solution for your specific business requirements.

In order to help you start and grow your business, Bizspace are offering one month's free virtual office or one month free in any of their units, dependent on a six-month signed agreement.

www.bizspace.co.uk

As part of their commitment to supporting entrepreneurs in the UK, Dell offers excellent technology advice and support through their website at www.dell.co.uk/solutions, including a free social media guide at www.dell.co.uk/business/socialmedia.

In addition, Dell are offering an extra £25 off when you spend £400 or more on a system from Dell's Vostro business laptop and desktop range. If the system you choose is less than £400, simply upgrade or add extra software such as Microsoft Office to activate the £25 discount.

To find out more about Dell's Vostro business range, visit www.dell.co.uk/vostro.

www.dell.co.uk

DHL is the global market leader in the logistics industry, committed to helping businesses grow at speed and with full support.

As part of this support, DHL are offering kit readers 10% off DHL Servicepoint at Staples Stores.

www.dhl.co.uk

Terms and conditions

1. All shipments are carried subject to DHL's Standard Terms and Conditions of Carriage.
2. This voucher entitles you, the customer, to a discount of 10% on one parcel sent from a participating Staples store to a destination within the DHL network. If you have multiple parcels, the most expensive parcel will receive the discount offer.
3. DHL and Staples cannot accept responsibility for the loss or theft of this voucher which cannot be reissued.
4. The discount cannot be used in conjunction with other promotional discount offers.
5. This voucher has no cash value and therefore cannot be refunded or exchanged for cash.
6. This voucher can only be used for a parcel from the UK. Only original vouchers can be accepted.
7. Offer ends 31st December 2013.

FreeAgent is one of the top online accounting systems available to start-ups, small businesses and freelancers both in the UK and overseas.

With FreeAgent's award-winning software you can:

- send professional invoices and automatically chase payments
- forecast tax commitments
- import bank statements and sort transactions
- manage expenses
- send estimates
- view real-time cash flow and profit & loss position
- submit VAT returns direct to HMRC
- automatically import data from your PayPal.

FreeAgent are extending a special offer in the StartUp Loans Kit which gives you three months free trial plus 10% off subscriptions to their great online accounting system.

www.freeagent.com

At HP we understand that technology is at the forefront of your business and it is because of this we aim to inform and collaborate with you to help businesses work better through technology. We have a keen focus providing SMEs with the tools they need to succeed, after all you drive the UK economy, and through the HP Business Answers group on LinkedIn we can help continue this momentum. We are always open to questions on technology for your business as well as anything else you need to know to drive your business forward.

The HP Business Answers group is a vibrant community of small and medium-sized business owners and employees. Every day, over 7,000 members are discussing best practice for businesses whether it's around design, networks, branding, taxation, technology, marketing or manufacturing. In just 12 months the group has grown to become a vital source of help and advice for its members.

Visit **www.linkedin.com/groups/HP-Business-Answers-3692681** to join the group, start a conversation and get access to the wealth of information that is already available.

As a start-up business, HP would also like to offer a little help with a 10% discount on the HP ProBook 4540s Notebook. To claim, simply visit the HP Online Store at **www.hp.com**, select the HP ProBook 4540s and then enter the discount code SAVE10SMB when you check out. The discount is available until 9 November 2012 or while stocks last.

www.hp.com

 **intuit.**

QuickBooks is the UK's No1 Accounting Software for small business. With no accounting knowledge necessary, QuickBooks easily organises everything in one place and saves you time on everyday bookkeeping tasks. With QuickBooks you can:

- easily create and personalise invoices
- monitor cash flow and keep on top of receivables
- file your VAT returns directly to HMRC – QuickBooks is always compliant with HMRC
- get the information you need with easy-to-use reports.

Getting started is a breeze too! You can quickly import you data from an Excel spreadsheet, and follow QuickBooks' guided set up – with step-by-step tutorials and coaching tips along the way.

Get started today and immediately begin to save time on your books, so you can focus on running your business – what really matters.

The QuickBooks *StartUp Loan Kit* offer gives you:

- 30 day free trial
- 20% saving on your software of choice
- 60-day money-back guarantee
- Free 'QuickBooks for Dummies' worth £17.99

That's a total saving of £89!

www.intuit.co.uk

Just-Eat.co.uk is the UK's leading online takeaway ordering service, providing a quick and convenient way to order food from local delivery restaurants.

With over 12,000 delivery restaurants throughout the UK, Just-Eat has a huge range of cuisines to choose from no matter what your taste, whether you're after a quick pizza delivery or gourmet Indian takeaway. Just-Eat also allows you to make great savings on your takeaway order, with more than 2,000 restaurants nationwide offering exclusive 20% discounts (or more!) for Just-Eat customers.

Orders placed on Just-Eat are digitally sent via Just-Eat's industry-leading JCT terminals, avoiding any misheard phone orders as well as allowing restaurant chefs to provide real-time order confirmation to you. And with secure, online card payments you can pay for your takeaway delivery without fishing for change at the bottom of your sofa.

Just-Eat are extending a special offer in *The StartUp Loan Kit* which gives you £3 off your next takeaway order.

www.just-eat.co.uk

KashFlow provides intuitive, easy-to-use accounting software for small business owners. It allows you to customise and edit invoices, as well as issuing them automatically. It'll even remind you when payment is overdue.

Kashflow also offers a free API and a ton of integration. If you're not technically minded, this just means it facilitates and automates lots of processes including PayPal payments, payroll, CRM and many more.

As well as being the leader in user-friendly accounting software, KashFlow is also a pioneer of the SaaS (software as a service) business model. This means it is based entirely online – there is no need to download anything, there are no clunky updates and no hidden charges. It also means you can access it on any computer that has internet access, so you can even check your accounts on a beach in Spain ... if you want to.

KashFlow is totally committed to customer retention. Because users pay a monthly fee rather than a lump sum, it strives to keep them happy, offering email support 24 hours a day, 7 days a week, 365 days a year.

KashFlow is extending a special offer in *The StartUp Loan Kit* which gives you three months' free trial of their great accounting system, instead of the standard 14-day trial.

www.kashflow.com

moo.com

MOO was born out of a love of beautiful, high-quality print. Since the launch of moo.com in 2006, we've worked hard to set a new standard for digital print, with remarkable new products that bring great design and uncompromisingly high standards to the web.

At MOO, we believe Business Cards should be a conversation starter, and we'd like to help your cards speak for themselves. With our Business Cards, and all other products, you can put a different image on every card or sticker you print. Have 50 different products for sale? Put images of all 50 of your products in one pack of Business Cards.

As an exclusive *StartUp Loan Kit* offer you can get 50 Classic or Green Business Cards from moo.com for FREE!*

www.moo.com

*Promo code valid for one use only before 31 May 2013. Just pay P&P on moo.com.

PAYPAL & EKMPOWERSHOP.COM

PayPal™

PayPal

PayPal is a fast and secure way for customers to pay you online using all major debit and credit cards, as well as online bank transfers and PayPal balance. Customers don't even need a PayPal account to pay you.

With 26 million accounts in the UK and over 230 million worldwide, PayPal is a popular payment method with millions of online shoppers and one of the global leaders in online payments.

PayPal offers a range of products to suit your business needs and size. Whether you want to accept payments directly on your site (Website Payments Standard), through a hosted PayPal page (Website Payments Pro), over the phone (Virtual Terminal) or via email (Email Payments), PayPal has a solution to meet your needs. Benefits include:

- no set-up or monthly fees – you only start paying when you start selling
- no approval required – start accepting online payments today
- chargeback protection on qualifying transactions
- you manage the entire customer relationship: customers return to your site to confirm payment, giving you another opportunity to engage them and encourage repeat business.

PayPal is the perfect solution for businesses in a wide range of industries, which will boost sales and expand your business.

www.paypal.co.uk

EKMPOWERSHOP.COM

ekmPowershop.com is the nation's leading ecommerce provider, powering one in every five online shops in the UK.

Clients using their market-leading ecommerce solution range from multinationals like PGA Golf, Michelin Tyres, Lotus Cars and O2 – through to independent retailers and tens of thousands of SMEs.

Online based with no technical knowledge or software required, ekmPowershop.com makes it easy for any business to set up and run an online shop.

Choose from a huge selection of stunning templates – and add your own logo, colour scheme and branding to make the shop front your own. Should you require a bespoke look and feel, ekmPowershop.com's also fully customisable.

ekmPowershop.com is fully integrated with PayPal's leading payment solution, meaning you can offer customers the most popular payment methods on the internet, all on your very own online shop.

With free support and no minimum term agreement, ekmPowershop.com really is the quickest and easiest way to set up your own online shop. There's no downloads or installation to worry about – all you need is an internet connection and some products to sell!

As part of the *StartUp Loan Kit*, PayPal and EKM are offering £1 for the first three months, to launch your complete ecommerce solution with no PayPal fees for 30 days. Once the three months expires, you pay only £19.99 per month with no contract.

www.ekmpowershop.com

Regus provides modern, flexible workspace that frees businesses of all sizes, all over the world, to work more effectively. Companies can take a fully-equipped office, desks to use part-time, come in to touch base or take advantage of a range of virtual office services.

Ready-to go: offices, meeting rooms and business lounges; the largest network of video communication studios in the world; reception facilities, virtual offices and a whole host of other business services. However you use Regus, you can get all the support a start-up or growing business needs.

That's space when you need it – but only when you need it; the room to expand as your business grows, with another fully-equipped office available overnight; elegant rooms for client meetings; a prestigious address and all the support that a business needs.

As part of their commitment to supporting small businesses, Regus are offering a great value **business start-up package** with savings of up to **£1,000**. The package includes an impressive business address, call answering and mail-handling services, professional business mentoring, business support services and discounts on meeting rooms. In addition, take advantage of access to drop-in business lounges offering an excellent place to meet and work with free Wi-Fi and tea/coffee.

www.regus.co.uk

Staples is the world's largest office products company and is committed to helping start ups and small business. It not only sells technology, office furniture and stationery but offers a wide range of business services.

15% off at Staples!

Everything you need to start and run a business!

Includes office supplies, printers, ink, paper, furniture – and don't forget Staples' Copy and Print Centre for your business cards, letterheads, envelopes, compliment slips …

www.staples.co.uk

Vistaprint has over 25 localised websites that serve various markets around the world, over 3,100 employees, three state of art manufacturing facilities and 13 offices. With over $2 billion in sales since 2006, Vistaprint is focused on giving the 50 million micro businesses around the world a chance to make an impression and stand out with professional marketing products and services at an affordable price.

Vistaprint, make an impression.

As part of their commitment to supporting small businesses, Vistaprint have two offers: 250 free business cards* and one month's free website trial.

www.vistaprint.co.uk

*Just pay P&P.